10-Minute Social Psychology

*The Critical Thinker's Guide to Social
Behavior, Motivation, and Influence
To Make Rational and Effective Decisions*

By
Albert Rutherford

services of a competent professional person should be sought. The author shall not be liable for damages arising herefrom. The fact that an individual, organization of website is referred to in this work as a citation and/or potential source of further information does not mean that the author endorses the information the individual, organization to website may provide or recommendations they/it may make. Further, readers should be aware that Internet websites listed in this work might have changed or disappeared between when this work was written and when it is read.

For general information on the products and services or to obtain technical support, please contact the author.

Written by Albert Rutherford

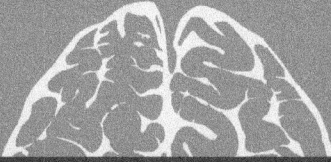

THE ART OF ASKING
POWERFUL QUESTIONS
IN THE WORLD OF SYSTEMS

FREE GIFT

WWW.ALBERTRUTHERFORD.COM

Visit www.albertrutherford.com to get your FREE GIFT: The Art of Asking Powerful Questions in the World of Systems

Table of Contents

Introduction

It goes without saying that human beings are social creatures. We thrive on social interaction with our family, friends, neighbors, coworkers, and any number of other individuals we interact with throughout the day. The social activities we engage in are what causes our brain to map out the biological reasons as well as the social and behavioral process of social neuroscience. This concept relies on biological reasons to develop theories on the social process, followed by neuroscience capturing the social aspects of behavior to refine and inform those theories.[i]

It's important to note that social neuroscience is not a concept reserved exclusively for humans, as animals that live in packs or groups share these behaviors as well. Consider the structure, interaction, and behavior of a wolfpack. Wolves have a deliberate hierarchy with both an alpha male and alpha female. Only the two alpha wolves are permitted to breed and have pups in the wolfpack structure. Then there is the beta wolf, which is only subordinate to the alpha wolf. Beta wolves are set to take over the job of alpha when the current alpha dies, and all of the remaining wolves in the pack are subordinate to both the alpha male and beta male.

The last remaining member of the pack's social structure is arguably one of the most important—the omega. Omega wolves are the weakest wolves in the pack and completely subordinate to all pack members. Omega wolves feed last or not at all if the alpha does not permit it, but pack members also engage in fights and intimidation to reduce stresses within the hierarchy of the wolfpack.[ii] The role of the omega is so significant within the social structure that when packs lose their omega, they stop hunting for a time so they can mourn their missing member. It's also important to note that omega wolves aren't forever doomed to remain an omega. The omega can fight his or her way up the hierarchy and even become the alpha wolf. This is not unheard of in wolfpack social structure.

It's clear that wolves have specific biological and behavioral requirements for interaction and hierarchy within their pack structure, but it's also clear that wolves have the potential to move into and out of different roles within those confines. Wolves are also not the only type of animal to engage in these kinds of behaviors. Killer whales and elephants are also well-researched, socially complex animals living in matriarchal social groups, and both display fascinating behavior and social interactions.

However, as humans, we are by far the most socially complex species on the planet, and social interaction is so important in human societies that many psychiatric disorders are viewed from the perspective of undesirable social behavior.[iii] Disorders such as personality disorders, social anxiety disorder, autism, and even attention deficient hyperactivity disorder are just a few examples of interrupted or abnormal social functioning classified as such in the *Diagnostic and Statistical Manual of Mental Disorders, 5th Edition*.

Social neuroscience was born from researchers' desire to understand how biology regulates and informs the social process and behavior. These social structures then impact both the brain and biology in return.[iv] As a means of gathering and analyzing this type of information, researchers John Cacioppo and Jean Decety created the international, interdisciplinary Society for Social Neuroscience.

The intent of this book is to introduce you to social neuroscience, how it impacts our daily lives as well as those around us, and how can we approach our gut-instincts with a pinch of critical thinking. We'll look at how the brain works in an effort to see where we can improve our lives and gain a better understanding of the complex social rituals in our society. So get ready to enjoy an informative and interesting book designed to help you understand social neuroscience and teach you what changes you can make to your social processes and biology to help you meet your goals. Open up your critical thinking brain wings, let's go!

Chapter 1: A Little Brain Anatomy

Phineas P. Gage was an American railroad worker who had the distinction of an iron railway bolt being driven straight through his head after an explosion, destroying much of his brain's frontal lobe.[v] Due to the damage to a significant part of Gage's brain, the iron rod buried deep inside his skull effectively altered his personality and behavior. Gage's friends often commented both of these aspects of Gage's life were so different after the accident, he was "no longer Gage."[vi]

Gage's accident took place in September 1848, and he only lived another 12 years after the accident occurred. However, Gage's experience of being impaled in the head by the iron rod inadvertently increased human understanding—it told us that brain cells have the ability to affect someone's personality, and damage to specific areas of the brain may lead to undesirable mental changes. Phineas Gage is such a shining example of how we humans rely on our brains to carry us through the simplest activities of everyday life. Gage's accident and subsequent mental changes are what led to him having roles in such areas as phrenology, psychology, and neuroscience.[vii]

Coincidentally, similar to the example of Gage's injury, the one and only time I have ever been selected as a juror in a criminal case involved the victim, a man in his 50s, attempting to break up a fight in the parking lot of a bar at closing. As the bar closed and the patrons emptied into the parking lot, two patrons who were known to dislike one another began to engage in the early stages of a physical altercation. The two men were loud, attempting to provoke the other, intoxicated, and clearly on a collision course to a fight. The victim, Jerry, stepped in between the two men in an attempt halt the action, but one of the aggressors subsequently punched him in the face so hard he fell to the pavement and struck his head.

Jerry suffered a traumatic brain injury that night, and despite his protestations otherwise, both Jerry's family and the surgeons and doctors who had tended to him testified to the severity and permanent effects of Jerry's injury. It was heartbreaking that a man who had tried to calm an explosive situation wound up permanently damaged for such foolish reasons, but Jerry's case is an example of how social neuroscience and social interactions can and do have a lasting effect on cognition and the brain.

One of the primary assumptions of social neuroscience is that all social behavior is put in to action biologically. This is the age-old question of nature versus nurture being asked yet again, and the answer here is nature. According to the Society for Social Neuroscience, the brain and human body have a significant impact on the function of social structures, such as families, neighborhoods, and even the impact of rural versus urban living. These various influences and experiences affect individuals due to the continuous mutual and reciprocal reactions between neural, neuroendocrine, metabolic, and immune factors on the brain and body. The brain is the central regulatory organ, but also the adaptive recipient of these factors.[viii]

To understand the complexities of social neuroscience and meaningfully think and talk about it –with a critical edge or otherwise -, it's important we start with understanding the structures and functions of the different parts of the human brain. For the purposes of social neuroscience, most of the research and discernible aspects of social cognition come from two large-scale subsets of the brain: the mirror neuron system (MNS) and the default mode network (DMN).[ix] Both of these subsets are further broken down into individual components, and we will discuss those as well as how they work together below.

Mirroring Neuron System (MNS)

Have you ever been told that you walk like your mom or look just like your dad when you're both surprised and excited? It's very common for specific behaviors such as how a person walks, expresses themselves, or drives their car to be transferred from one person to another. Essentially, one person picks up these actions and behaviors from others around them and "mirrors" them, adapting them into their own actions and behaviors.[x] One of the reasons we see this "mirroring" in families is because these are often the people who teach us, but also have a consistent presence in our lives for us to follow.

This gives a whole new concept to the idea of role modeling, doesn't it? People learn by copying what they observe, and this is one of the reasons we, as a society, talk about stopping the cycle of domestic violence. We need to model that these violent and destructive behaviors are abnormal and teach observable components of a healthy relationship and conflict resolution. Many children who grow up in households where domestic violence is present grow up thinking those behaviors occur in every family. By the time the child has grown and matured enough to realize the behaviors are not normal, they have observed the violence, and that method of conflict resolution is somewhat ingrained in them.

This is not to suggest that all victims of domestic violence or other types of abuse become abusers themselves. We know that is not true, but we also know that there is a cycle and pattern of behavior that can be passed down from one generation to the next. Even something as simple as childhood discipline can and does have a lasting impact on individuals well into their adult years and long after childhood discipline disappears. One of the biggest parenting debates in existence is whether or not parents should or should not use corporal punishment, or spanking, in their discipline toolkit.

Numerous longitudinal research studies have shown that spanking can cause increased levels of aggression, depression, and low self-esteem among children and adults. These are just a few of the negative effects researchers have found regarding the use of spanking in child rearing. However, many adults will simply tell you they were spanked as children themselves and they turned out just fine. I can't tell you how to raise your children, but considering what we know about mirrored behaviors, it's worth thinking about how the behaviors parents model will affect not just children, but grandchildren and great grandchildren. Social science has come a long way in showing us that previously acceptable behaviors, such as beating your spouse, are harmful and destructive and not to be tolerated.

It is also important to note that there is some controversy among researchers as to whether or not mirroring neurons exist in the human MNS, as much of the research has been conducted on macaque monkeys. Because some scientists argue there is no definitive proof of mirroring neurons in the

MNS, the MNS is sometimes referred as the action observation network, action identification network, or the action representation network. There are other competing theories of what stimulates the motor function in humans and classical theories look at different aspects than newer ones that are cognition based.

Anatomy of the MNS[xi]

Premotor cortex – Mirror neurons were first discovered in this part of the brain, and it is the part of the brain responsible for autonomic movements, such as breathing, as well as processing language and comprehension of actions. The mirroring neurons are responsible for the brain's response to acquiring language as well as producing speech. The premotor cortex also aids in how individuals engage in multiple actions at one time and even the ordering of those actions to achieve the desired outcome.

If we think about the premotor cortex in terms of how we learn and process language and speech, one way we can see this in action is through the use of dialects and accents. In the US, geographic regions are often associated with a particular way of speaking, accent, or drawl. I grew up in the Southeastern United States, and so I have the typical accent accompanying that region. When I travel to other regions, people will sometimes ask me about it if they are unfamiliar with my accent and pronunciation.

Another well-known accent in the US is the Boston accent. There are many running jokes of that area's use of the "ah" sound in place of a hard rolling R sound. One example is the sentence, "Park the car in Harvard Yard." Someone with a Bostonian accent may pronounce these words as, "Pahk the cah in Hahvahd Yahd." One of the funnier examples of language and speech is how to properly pronounce the word pecan. Is it pee-can or pa-kahn? Well, that depends on where you're from and how you learned to speak. My mother would tell you a "pee-can" is a not a nut that you eat, but rather a receptacle or urine, and she wants no part of that. Therefore, we enjoy "pa-kahn" pie during the holidays.

Intraparietal sulcus (IPS)[xii]– This part of the brain is responsible for sensorimotor mirroring. The IPS is responsible for such tasks as eye and arm movements as well as understanding numerical magnitude processing. This is important, as impairments in the IPS have been shown to have a correlation in math-related learning disabilities. Studies have even shown that children who have these types of learning disabilities, known as dyscalculia, have a smaller amount of gray matter in their left IPS. The IPS is also what helps individuals understand magnitude and how it relates in all the various roles of a person's life. The understanding of magnitude moves beyond how it relates to numbers and number processing as it helps individuals understand differences based on terms such as upper class, middle class, and working class, for example.

Lateral occipitotemporal cortex (LOTC) – This part of the MNS is also responsible for sensorimotor mirroring; visual processing and the representation of abstract action is also housed here. When you think about the LOTC, think about areas of the body that are sensitive to movement, the kinetics of body parts and movement, and even posture as well. One way we see social cues affect the LOTC is through the use of cellphones. Individuals who spend a significant amount of time looking down at a cellphone in their hands often sit or stand in a position that causes their head to move forward and slump down, rolling the neck and shoulders forward. This habitual lack of standing up straight and maintaining good posture can lead to the development of a kyphosis, or hump, in the upper back that starts to present at increasingly younger ages. If our society keeps moving forward in this manner, the average adult may start to resemble Quasimodo in their 20s or 30s.

Default Mode Network (DMN)[xiii]

This subset of the brain is where more of the abstract activities and ideas are housed. The DMN is responsible for things like social interactions, intent, and traits. This is the part of the brain that allows and regulates our emotions, morals, and sense of recognition of these same characteristics in others. The DMN is the hub of human social cognition. Without the DMN we would also not be able to experience the concept of a daydream, or when a person lets their mind wander or simply gets lost in thought. Imagination is one of the key parts of human behavior we see emerge from this part of the brain.

As a kindergarten teacher, I work with very young children, who are usually a force unto themselves in terms of their creativity and imagination. This year alone, I have only just learned about the "existence" of alicorns, a winged unicorn, and llamacorns, a llama that is also a unicorn. It never ceases to amaze me the different things children come up with. Our class worked on a story a while ago, and the setting the children chose for the story was in the state of Florida, deep in the forest, inside the tip of a pencil. Who am I to stop that creativity?

However, one day several weeks ago, I had asked the children to draw, from their imagination, the beginning, middle, and ending ideas of a story they want to tell. After a few minutes, I noticed one of the children sitting quietly, not participating in the activity, and staring forlornly off into the middle distance. I asked the girl what was the matter and why she wasn't drawing out the parts of her story. The little girl motioned for me to bend down so she could whisper in my ear. She said, "Ms. S, don't tell anyone, but I don't have an imagination."

I couldn't help myself and busted out laughing as this little girl has such a vivid imagination. After we talked about it for a few minutes, she was able to see her creativity and enthusiastically work on the task. One of the reasons this child may have gone into a state of confusion is that the DMN is often activated when we are at rest and the brain isn't working toward a specific goal. Because the student was so focused on the task and its completion, she may have temporarily blocked out her creative flow. I thought of it as something similar to writer's block, which is when writers find themselves experiencing the inability to create new work or have a significant slowing of their creative ideas.

Because individuals often experience these aspects of social cognition and activity when they are at rest and their brain isn't actively working toward goal completion, it is often thought of as the "default mode" of the brain. Hence the name of these parts of the brain, which are discussed in greater detail below. Researchers and scientists don't really understand why or how all of these different parts of the DMN work together, but it is believed there is some underlying connection.

Anatomy of the DMN[4]

<u>Medial prefrontal cortex (mPFC)</u> – This part of the brain is associated with mentalization, which is the ability to understand one's own mental status as well as the mental status of others. The mPFC is highly used when mentalizing about others, but less so when examining one's own mental status. This part

of the brain is also used in social cognition as it allows individuals to examine and determine the affective components of others, such as their mood or how their feeling. This is also the part of the brain that allows humans to evaluate the goodness or badness of an event or stimulus. So, if you're one of the many people who have ever had a "gut feeling" about a situation, this is your mPFC kicking in.

Posterior cingulate cortex (PCC) – The role of the PCC in social cognition and neuroscience is not yet well known or understood, though it is believed to be tightly interwoven with the mPFC. It is hypothesized that the PCC may be responsible for tracking social dynamics as it uses external environmental cues and stimuli to guide a person's attention based on what is occurring in the background. The PCC is linked to how individuals to adapt and undergo behavioral changes in response to their environment. This is believed to aid in social navigation.

Temporoparietal Junction (TPJ) – This is a very important part of the human brain, as the TPJ is what helps people separate the different entities in any given situation. The TPJ is what helps you determine yourself from others. The TPJ is also responsible for your ability to separate your own ideas and beliefs from those of others. We depend on the TPJ for such tasks as reorienting our attention, updating context, and retrieving episodic memories. The TPJ is critical to social cognition, and without it, we would likely find ourselves melting aspects of our personalities into others' due to an inability to regulate false belief tasks.

Superior temporal sulcus (STS) – Parts of the STS are responsible for our perceptual inputs and entering those into the DMN, while other parts of the STS take on the tasks of abstract thinking in the social context and identifying person-related information.

Additional Anatomy[xiv]

In the realm of social neuroscience, the brain also houses other structures that significantly contribute to social cognition. These areas include the following:

Ventrolateral prefrontal cortex (VLPFC) – This part of the brain is linked to emotional and inhibition response processing. This is what helps us assess a person's facial expression and convert that information into understanding their emotional response in that moment. The VLPFC is also responsible for assessing body language and displaying empathy and mentalizing.

Insula – The insula is a requisite component in the processing of emotions as well as one's own internal state of the body. Without the insula, individuals would find it difficult to assess if they were having a medical emergency, such as a heart attack, or even if they were struggling from a mental illness such as anorexia or bulimia. The insula may also be responsible for the feeling of pain affiliated with social rejection.

Anterior cingulate cortex (ACC) – The ACC shares some of its roles with the insula, such as regulating emotional processing. Specifically, the ACC is thought to be the focus of processing negative emotions, such as the pain of social rejection, as well as determining negative social thoughts in others. On the flip side, the ACC may also engage in activating vicarious rewards, which is the repetition of behaviors that others are rewarded for, which is considered a beneficial social behavior.

Fusiform face area (FFA) – The FFA is where individuals process the faces of others, including visuospatial features, and the perceptions that arise from that processing.

Brainwaves[xv]

Now that we understand all of the different parts of the brain that facilitate social cognition, we need to know a little about brainwaves, or neural oscillations, to prepare us for the remaining chapters in this book. Brainwaves are rhythmic and repeating patterns of neurological activity in the central nervous system. Brain tissue generates brainwaves in many ways and are guided by mechanisms within individual neurons or interactions between those neurons.

In individual neurons, the wave can appear as oscillations in membrane potential or as patterns of action potentials, which then activate the wave of post-synaptic neurons. At the level of neural groupings, contemporaneous activity of large numbers of neurons can create macroscopic oscillations, which are observable in an electroencephalogram. Wave activity in sets of neurons is generated from feedback connections between the neurons, resulting in the synchronization of their firing patterns. Interaction between neurons can cause the brainwaves to occur at a different frequency than the firing frequency of individual neurons.

Specific Brainwave Types

<u>Delta wave</u>[xvi] – Delta waves have a high amplitude and a low frequency. Amplitude is a measure of the size of the wave's vibration,

whereas frequency is a measure of how often the wave occurs. Delta waves most often occur in non-REM sleep, and will begin to appear in sleep stage 3. However, by stage 4, nearly all brainwaves have become delta waves. Interestingly, across mammals of all species, females tend to have more delta waves than their male counterparts. Though, in humans, this does not become evident until a person reaches their 30s or 40s.

Theta wave[xvii] – The theta rhythm has a regularly appearing sine curve and generally appears at a slower frequency. Theta waves are generated from the hippocampal region of the brain and are generally recorded from humans in REM sleep. Theta waves generated by humans are called cortical theta rhythms and are read from electrodes placed on the scalp. Theta waves in other mammals experience a stronger oscillation known as the hippocampal theta rhythm. There have been studies of humans with hippocampal theta rhythms, but these studies have been small and related to epilepsy patients with intracranial electrode implants.

Alpha wave[xviii] – There are several different types of alpha waves, but these waves occur at a higher frequency than delta and theta waves, and alpha wave amplitude is affected by numerous factors. They come from the occipital lobe during times of wakeful relaxation, but are generated by the frontal-central area of the brain during REM sleep. There has been some recent speculation that alpha waves during wakeful relaxation are actually coming from the thalamus. There is some suggestion of a link between alpha waves and fibromyalgia, as patients with fibromyalgia often experience the occurrence of alpha waves during stage 4 sleep, when delta waves are supposed to be present.

Beta wave[xix] – Beta waves have a high frequency, higher than alpha waves, and are associated with waking consciousness. They do have a lower amplitude than other waves, which is affected by the individual's activities, the pace of those activities, and even anxiety.

Gamma wave[xx] – Gamma waves occur at the highest frequency of the brainwaves discussed in this chapter. Gamma waves are linked to large-scale brain activity such as attention, cognition, and memory. There has been some controversy surrounding gamma waves, as some scientists doubt their validity as detected through electrodes placed on the scalp due to the gamma wave frequency overlapping with the frequency of the EEG. Gamma wave disruption is also linked to mood and cognitive disorders like Alzheimer's disease and schizophrenia.

The purpose of this short neurobiology class was to help you have a basic knowledge of these brain regions. When you read an article mentioning Gamma waves, for example, you can understand better what the article is about and do critical reading and critical questioning with more authority. We need to know, get familiar, and deeply understand topics before we start questioning them or forming strict opinions of them. Before we gain that authority, it's advised to have a question mark at the end of our sentences.

Chapter 2: Social Psychology

Social psychology is the study of how peoples' thoughts, feelings, and behavior are affected by the influence of others. Interestingly, it is important to note that a person does not have to actually have to be in the presence of another person and can be completely alone for this influence to take place.[xxi] For example, when I was in high school, the movie *Clueless* was released, starring Alicia Silverstone. The movie is a coming-of-age story about a wealthy high school girl living in Beverly Hills, CA. The main character's persona is that of a stereotypical "valley girl" and she speaks and uses phrases one would associate with that persona.

After the release of the movie, many of the girls in my high school adopted the valley girl persona, and it became common to hear phrases from the movie like "as if," "oh my god, I'm totally buggin'," or "that was way harsh." None of these phrases had been used in my school prior to the release of that film, but simply viewing the movie, in the presence of others or alone, influenced the behavior and speech of the girls in my entire high school. Even those that had not seen the movie were subsequently influenced by this newly adopted language being used in their presence, and so we see social psychology at work.

Another aspect of social psychology is that the behaviors do not even have to occur in order have an influence on others. It is more than possible for implied or imagined thoughts, feelings, and behavior to impact an individual's behavior.[xxii] Another Hollywood example is that of the character Dexter Morgan from the Showtime TV series, *Dexter*, and even more so the books written by Jeff Lindsey, such as *Darkly Dreaming Dexter*, which were the inspiration for the series. Dexter Morgan, the main character, is a serial killer with a heart of gold in that he only kills criminals who have committed horrible crimes and are a threat to society.

In the novel *Darkly Dreaming Dexter*, Dexter specifically discusses how he "reads" people in social interactions in an attempt to copy their behavior in an effort to fit into the crowd of humanity and not stand out. He is essentially a wolf attempting to hide in the clothing of normal behavior. The book and TV series clearly show scenes that make Dexter feel awkward and out of place, but because he knows the value of fitting in, he fakes his way through these social interactions. In contrast, when Dexter messes up and misinterprets social interactions and feelings, it provides some much needed levity to the dark nature of his character.

The goal of social psychology is to understand how a given set of factors unfold in social situations and study the conditions that lead to certain behaviors, thoughts, goals, and interactions. Social psychology researchers strive to understand how these cognitions are created and then subsequently how they affect others through social interaction. Once upon a time, in the era immediately following World

War II, social psychology was a discipline meant to fill in the gap between psychology and sociology.[xxiii] As time has passed, these disciplines have continued to become more and more specific unto themselves. Despite this, it is undeniable that sociological constructs have an influence on psychology, and social psychologists focus their research in this area.

Intrapersonal Phenomena

Intrapersonal phenomena refers to a person's innate feelings and attitudes about themselves and also includes the self-concept. In addition to attitude and self-concept, social cognition and persuasion are also components of intrapersonal phenomena. We will discuss each of these areas more in depth below.

Attitude – Attitudes are defined as learned global evaluations of a person, thought, object, or situation that has an impact on a person's thoughts or actions.[xxiv] Attitudes are how we demonstrate our opinions on any given thing, our likes and dislikes. A simple example of an attitude is my dislike of fish. There's no beating around the bush when it comes to food, I hate fish. I wish I didn't dislike it because it's healthy, low in calories, high in protein, and just a good food choice when not fried. I've tried hard to like fish, experimented with different flavors and fish of different textures, but I still don't like it. I've given up on ever enjoying a dish made from fish, and my attitude toward it is just who I am as a person. I can't change this aspect of myself despite my many attempts to do so.

Attitudes cannot always provide an explanation for a specific behavior, as there are times when, despite a person's attitude, they may choose to operate outside their specific likes and dislikes. Taking the example of fish from above, I have gone to a restaurant and ordered a fish dish off the menu by choice. That is a really weird decision by someone who clearly doesn't enjoy fish, so what would make me do this? In the situation where this has happened, I was out at a business dinner with my husband's company. Due to the large number of guests, the company had preset a menu where the primary entree was either beef, shrimp, or a stuffed fish fillet. As I had attended this dinner in years prior, I'd already had the beef and shrimp dishes and hadn't enjoyed them for various reasons. On the evening I ordered the fish, I thought it was a toss-up as to what I ordered because I was simply not likely to enjoy that part of the meal. I ultimately decided to order the fish because I wanted to eat the seafood stuffing inside the fillet, which was really tasty.

It's not exactly clear how attitudes are formed, but according to Abraham Tesser, these traits are part of our genetic make-up.[xxv] Tesser believes that how we feel about certain topics, our temperament, how we think in social situations, and our personality traits are essentially a result of our parents' DNA coming together to create us. It's true that attitudes can be learned and certain cherished beliefs, ideas, and many of our attitudes are influenced by outside sources such as societal norms, the beliefs of friends and family, and culture. Some people even form extreme positive or negative attitudes about neutral objects based on learned attitudes. An example might be a person who fears taking any kind of oral medication, even medicine needed to cure or treat illness, because they grew up in a household with a parent addicted to prescription painkillers.

Persuasion - Persuasion is an active and guided attempt to lead someone to adopting a specific idea, behavior, or attitude by using emotions or rational argument. To be clear, persuasion is not an attempt to coerce or pressure someone, as it relies on an attempt to entreaty others into taking a particular view. Any number of varying factors influence the process of persuasion, many of which fall into five categories: the communicator, the message, the audience, the channel, and the context.[xxvi]

1. *The communicator* – When it comes to persuasion, factors that create influence from the communicator include things such as trustworthiness, how attractive the person is, whether or not they are an

expert on the topic, and an evaluation of the communicator's credibility. It is often said that former president John Kennedy won the 1960 presidential election because of the first televised presidential debates. The turning point in the election came during the first debate. Nixon, who had recently been hospitalized, was seen to be pale and underweight. He sweated a lot under the lights on the stage, and because he didn't wear makeup, his five o'clock shadow was prominent. He looked sick, unkempt, and shifty in his television debut, and it cost him the election.

2. *The message* – Factors that influence the message include whether or not the message is reasonable—sometimes emotions, such as hate, are used—and any other source of information to back up claims are often common components of a strong persuasive

message. One prominent example is the Westboro Baptist Church. The Westboro Baptist Church is unequivocally a hate group, and they regularly spend their time protesting events, funerals, and organizations in conflict with their beliefs. After the 2016 Pulse Nightclub terror attack, the Westboro Baptist Church publicly celebrated the deaths of 49 people and the injury of 53 others, all members of the LGBTQ+ community. Their claim was that the attack was God's punishment against the members of this community, and others who share their beliefs may be persuaded to join their "congregation" based on their hateful message.

3. *The audience* – Knowing information about those you are trying to persuade is an invaluable piece of information, as it helps you construct your argument around the

demographics and preferences of the group. Trying to persuade the members of a steak-of-the-month club to adopt a vegan lifestyle is not likely to go as well as making that same appeal to a group of vegetarians.

4. *The channel* – The channel refers to how the attempt to persuade is made. Are you attempting to persuade people to come to your restaurant for dinner? Then using a TV ad with images of your food and a fun or intimate atmosphere may be more successful that a radio spot. The channel can include print items like posters or flyers, conversation, and the internet as well.

5. *The context* – The context of the situation includes aspects of the environment, group dynamics, and other factors surrounding the purpose of the message. One of the controversial arguments in favor of

more laws for gun control is the context that when the second amendment to the Constitution was written, there were no federally funded military branches, as the US was still in its infancy as a country. The argument is that because we now have national military branches, there should be changes to the second amendment allowing for limitations on gun ownership.

Social cognition – Social cognition is a newer area of social psychology that examines how individuals think about, perceive, and remember things about other people. The idea is that people think about others differently than they do non-social targets. One of the significant areas of research in social cognition is attributions, or the explanations we give to peoples' behavior, including our own. For example, my two-year-old is having a tantrum because he's overtired. Attributions can include internal factors such as personality traits, character, and disposition.[xxvii] An example of an internal attribution is my inclination to return a lost wallet to its owner because it's the right thing to do.

There are also external attributions, which consist of an almost endless list of factors that influence individuals. This includes factors like socioeconomic status, traffic, or having a cold, just to name a few. I came home from work last night in a foul mood because I spent two hours stuck in bumper-to-bumper traffic on the freeway is an example of an external attribution. I might have also worked a double shift and had a runny nose, contributing to my mood and my reactions to my family.

There are a number of biases associated with attributions as well. Many of these concern protecting the inner self and explaining away behavior that makes us vulnerable or forces us to examine our own mortality in place of a simple explanation preventing such worrisome examination. One example is blaming others for your problems rather than seeing how your own actions caused you to end up in a bind. It's a lot easier to say that your power got cut off because you didn't get enough hours at work or because your car insurance went up than it is to say you couldn't afford to pay your power bill because you called in sick Monday because you were hungover and your car insurance went up because you got a speeding ticket.

One of the other key concepts in social cognition is an accurate assessment of reality. Reality is truly complex and so, as humans, we create simplified versions of reality that shade how we see the world. One way that we do this through stereotypes. Stereotypes have a grain of truth in them, but we know they are really overly generalized assumptions we make about a group of people. Some common stereotypes we either face or even propagate on a daily basis include Asians are good at math, girls aren't good at sports, Jews are greedy. It doesn't take a lot of personal experience or even research to delve into these stereotypes and find out they are grossly misrepresentative of an entire population of people. Another way we simplify reality is by creating scripts for certain behaviors, such as grocery shopping, walking the dog, or even washing the dishes.

<u>Self-concept</u> – Generally speaking, self-concept encompasses the entirety of the beliefs a person has about themselves. However, according to Hazel Markus, self-concept is really a group of cognitive molecules used to create self-schemas. Self-schemas are made up of the beliefs we have about ourselves, and in turn, guide how we process self-reliant information.[xxviii] One example of self-schemas would be a working mother and all the different identities, or selves, housed in this single person.

A working mother would have an employee self, who undertakes the roles of her job to make sure it is getting done currently and efficiently; a parenting self that ensures her children are fed a nutritious dinner, get to school on time, and are given kisses each night they are tucked into bed; and possibly a partner self, who she allows to share her dreams with, like a significant other, engaging in sexual activity with that partner, and also helping maintain the family unit with that partner. All of these different selves have particular roles in this one person's life, but it is the individual "selves" that direct actions and behaviors to ensure the roles are completed correctly.

In our individual worlds, the self holds a place of highest regard. Our attention is most often directed back at ourselves. The value of self-concept is so important that extensive research has been conducted on the topic. Most of the research focuses on the cognitive piece of self-concept, the self-schema, as well as an evaluative piece, self-esteem. In the field of social psychology, maintaining a healthy self-esteem is viewed as the primary human motivation.[xxix]

Interpersonal Phenomena

If intrapersonal phenomena are the innate feelings and attitudes we have about ourselves, interpersonal phenomena represent the feelings and attitudes we hold from outside influences. Our relationships and communication with others affect the areas of interpersonal attraction, group dynamics, and social influence, which are discussed in more depth below.

<u>Interpersonal attraction</u> – Interpersonal attraction refers to all the forces that cause people to like one another, establish relationships, and even fall in love.[xxx] It is our relationships with others that can cause us to behave in both prosocial and antisocial ways. Interpersonal attraction may cause us to help our would-be partner in ways we most definitely would not assist someone we weren't attracted to. The comedian Ali Wong, in her Netflix stand-up special *Baby Cobra*, hilariously jokes about how she "landed" her husband. One of her clever strategies was making her boyfriend's lunch for him every day. She states that by helping him, she hoped he would become dependent on her and ask her to marry him. While this is all in jest, doing things for others to build and strengthen relationships is a prosocial aspect of interpersonal attraction, just ask anyone who

has helped their best friend move a couch into their three-story walk-up apartment.

It is also possible to behave antisocially due to interpersonal attraction. This could be the quintessential jealous boyfriend or jealous girlfriend. Jealousy is a strong emotion and people have gotten into fights with innocent parties over it and even killed over their attraction to their partner. One rather famous case of extreme jealousy is that of Elizabeth "Betty" Broderick's 1989 murders of her ex-husband, Dan, and his new wife, Linda, as they slept peacefully in their bed. Betty had financially supported Dan and their children through both law school and medical school. After his completion of his degrees and success as a medical malpractice attorney, Dan divorced Betty in order to continue an affair with his assistant, Linda Kolkena.

Dan and Betty's divorce was contentious and took four years to resolve, during which time Betty's behavior became increasingly violent and erratic. This included defying a restraining order Dan had taken out against Betty, preventing her from coming onto his property. Betty drove her car into the front door of Dan's house, despite the fact her own children were inside. Dan and Linda were married in 1989, just after the divorce was finalized, and Betty killed them both after less than six months. Betty's insane jealousy of Dan and his new wife were the antisocial behaviors that led to a double murder.

Group Dynamics – Groups are defined as two or more people connected together through social relationships. When individuals in the group interact, they influence one another, and most groups share a common identity. Groups are important parts of an individual's life because they are often a source of social support, resources, and they help the individual form a self-identity. Many people define themselves by the groups they belong to. Additionally, many groups have clear norms, roles, and relations.[xxxi]

> a. Norms are the implied rules that all the members are expected to follow.

b. Roles refers to the specific expectations for particular members of the group.
c. Relations are the patterns within the group that show liking, differences in status, or leadership within the group.

One example of these different qualities in a group setting is that of the Italian-American mafia. Mafia families have very clear-cut norms for existing within their unit. Some of these rules include only those members of Italian descent are permitted to become "made" guys, getting permission from the boss before carrying out a hit, and the concept of omerta—the refusal to discuss crimes or rat out others to the authorities. Roles within a mafia family include soldiers, capos, consigliere, underboss, and boss. Each of these roles have particular responsibilities and perks associated with them, and not staying within the confines of your assigned role could be a deadly offense. Mafia families also show their preference for certain members by moving them up in the ranks from soldier to capo or capo to consigliere. Often, the consigliere is the boss's most trusted advisor.

Social Influence – Social influence is defined by how others impact the thoughts, feelings, and behaviors of others—as a result, there is a lot of overlap in the research on social influence, attitudes, and persuasion. Social influence and group dynamics are also closely related, as a lot of social influences occurs within groups. The three main aspects of social influence are conformity, obedience, and compliance.[xxxii] There have been a number of fascinating psychological studies on these aspects, and we will discuss some of those in depth later in this book.

Another area of social influence is the self-fulfilling prophecy. The self-fulfilling prophecy is based on a set of expectations that in turn cause the individual to behave in such a way that the expectation occurs. Have you ever walked into a job interview with the expectation you will get the position? Because you are confident the job is yours, your answers are on point, you have a personality that displays a fit for the company culture, and you are relaxed and poised as you meet all your new coworkers and the boss. Because you performed so well in the interview, the company calls the following week to offer you the job. This is a perfect example of the self-fulfilling prophecy.

Methods: Social Psychology versus Social Neuroscience

Social Psychology – The methodology practiced by social scientists in both lab and field settings involve the use of empirical science to test hypotheses and answer questions about human behavior. Out of the necessity to produce high-quality studies, social psychologists pay special attention to experimental design, sampling, and their statistical analysis. High-quality studies that are planned and executed carefully are often published in peer-reviewed journals, which for those researchers working in academia, is vital to tenure and promotion. Social psychologists have a preference for controlled studies, where they manipulate independent variables to measure the effect on a dependent variable.[xxxiii]

Most studies in social psychology will use either experimental methods, observational methods, or correlational methods. Experimental methods are used to measure how a specific variable is affected by an environmental variable. Observational methods are strictly descriptive and take place in the individual's natural setting. Correlational methods measure the statistical association between two naturally occurring variables.[xxxiv] If we look at each of these methods to examine the uptick in shark attacks when there is also an increase in ice cream sales in our beachside town, these would be the difference between different methodologies:

Experimental: Purchasing the same amount of ice cream from local vendors every day for thirty days to evaluate the occurrence of shark attacks during that same thirty-day period.

Observational: Unobtrusively video recording the beach and oceanfront to examine behaviors of beach goers and swimmers on days when shark attacks occur and whether or not they are eating ice cream.

Correlational: Examining all the shark attacks in the area over a twelve-month period and reviewing the total ice cream sales during the same period to discover the statistical relationship between ice cream sales and shark attacks.

<u>Social Neuroscience</u> – Because of the biological component of social neuroscience that is not present in social psychology, methods practiced in social neuroscience experimentation often rely on the use of imaging and equipment used to measure brain activity. This equipment can include fMRI scans, PET scans, NIRS caps, and EEGs just to name a few.[xxxv] This is hardly an exhaustive list of technology used in social neuroscience. It is important to note that each of the tests and measures used to evaluate biological activity in the brain and how it is affected by

behavioral events can only provide correlational data.

In social science there is a research phrase many scientists firmly believe in: correlation doesn't equal causation. However, most social neuroscience studies cannot prove causation because there are any number of other factors that could contribute to the study's findings. Something as simple as another stimulus in the room or even the subject's thoughts can trigger brain activity, and scientists cannot be certain of the exact cause of their data. [xxxvi]

Many social neuroscience experiments rely on their test subject to self-report data. This is such an invaluable method for scientists because they are able to better understand what was happening to the test subject during the experiment. One exception to the limitations of social neuroscience studies is that studies examining hormones are able to infer causation by administering a particular hormone to the test group and a placebo to the control group. In addition to self-reported measures, many social neuroscience studies rely on observational methods and performance-based measures (response time or accuracy), which are all primarily psychological methods.[xxxvii]

The Asch Experiments[xxxviii]

The Asch conformity experiments are one type of the fascinating psychological studies mentioned previously in this book. The studies were completed by Dr. Soloman Asch and were designed to measure how people would conform to a majority group, even if the group was incorrect. In the Asch studies, all of the participants except the individual being evaluated were actors. The actors understood the true purpose of the study, but the test subject did not. Subjects were asked to look at a card with a reference line. Participants were then asked to look at another card with three lines, two of which were obviously shorter or longer than the reference line. Participants were then asked to state aloud which line was the same length as the reference sample.

The actors in the group all agreed prior to the start of each experiment which line they were going to report as matching the reference sample. In some cases, the actors' response would be correct and in others it would be intentionally incorrect. The experiments were designed in such a way that each test subject would always provide their response last. Each test subjects underwent the experiment eighteen times. On the first and second run-throughs, all of the actors gave correct responses followed by an incorrect response in the third trial. The remaining fifteen trials were then used to measure the question of the study: How many times would the test subject change their answer to provide a conforming response? Eleven of the remaining fifteen trials provided the obviously incorrect response, and these eleven trials combined with the third trial (first incorrect response) made up the twelve critical trials of the study.

The results of the study showed that in the control group, those experiments where a test subject underwent no pressure to provide a specific response, the error rate was less than

1%. However, in the test group, 36.8% of test subjects conformed to the majority response provided by the actors, and 75% of all test subjects gave at least one incorrect answer in response to pressure from the actors.

The debriefing interviews of the test subjects provided significant information into why tests subjects who had responded incorrectly had done so. Many of them reported that they did not actually believe the conforming response to be correct, but they were afraid of being ridiculed or thought of as weird. However, there were some test subjects who stated they truly believed the incorrect response was indeed correct. This told Asch that people primarily conform to the group for two major reasons: because they want to fit in and because they think the group is more well-informed than they are.

Chapter 3: Cooperation versus Competition

A number of years ago, in the spring when the weather started to warm up and we could all stand to be outside longer than two minutes, I enrolled my son, David, on a soccer team for toddlers. It was one of the earliest age groups the children could begin playing, and I thought he'd enjoy running around outside and making new friends. The first evening I took him to soccer practice was an unmitigated disaster. The class was huge and meant to be divided into what would become two soccer "teams" of three- and four-year-old kids. Herding toddlers is somewhat akin to herding cats. It's impossible, and this is where I got a good look into the value of learning the skills of cooperation and competition.

The kids were a hilarious mess of those who were faster and more agile and those who seemed like they had never seen a ball before. The faster and more agile children were able to monopolize the soccer ball, kicking it far into the distance and then running after it to keep up their momentum as they headed toward makeshift goals. The kids who were slower and more clumsy—ahem, David— would gently nudge the ball with their feet only to have one of the more agile children swoop in and kick it away from them. As the clumsy children chased after their ball in a haze of wails and tears, many of them would fall or even face-plant into the grass. Don't worry, no one was injured in the making of these future soccer champions.

But that's why they call it soccer practice, right? Faithfully, I took David to practice twice each week, and gradually over the season, he got better. He learned how to kick the ball to another person and receive a kicked ball in turn, and by the end of the season he was moderately fast and moderately agile. The season culminated in a game between the two toddler soccer teams formed on the first night. It was a beautiful thing to watch as a parent. Over the course of the season, not only did my child's skill improve as a competitor as he learned how to guard the ball from more adept players, but he also learned how to cooperate with the other children on his team in an effort to win the game.

In today's society, team sports is one of the quintessential ways we can actively watch both competition and cooperation occurring in tandem. The players on the same team are all working together, capitalizing on the skills of each individual player, to score points in the game while simultaneously competing against their counterparts on the other team. In football, the one team is on the offensive, trying to keep up the forward momentum of the ball toward the end zone. Football players use blocking, tackling, pulling, and sweeping to allow their quarterback and receivers to score points. On the defense, players rush, blitz, and use zone defense strategies to prevent the opposing team from scoring.

In terms of social cognition, cooperation is defined as maximizing outcomes for the benefit of yourself and others. In contrast, competition is the maximization of an advantage over others, which generally only provides benefits to yourself. It should be noted that cooperation and competition don't exist in a vacuum isolated from one another. In fact, much like team sports, they often occur together. While there have been a number of research experiments on cooperation and competition, the heart of cooperation is to find the solution to a problem that benefits everyone.

As we've already discussed, people have innate qualities that are driven, in part, by their genetic make-up. Much like personality, the desire and willingness to cooperate seems to be more prevalent in some people than it is in others. These cooperative people are know as prosocials. Studies on prosocials have shown that they are more likely to be part of a large group of siblings, make self-sacrifices for the good of their close relationships, and even make donations to what they consider to be worthy causes. Prosocial individuals also put more value in the inherent goodness of people. They are more willing to cooperate with others because they have a high level of trust for people in general.

One of the tools used by prosocials is norms. Norms are highly influential, and they often include a set of prescribed acceptable responses in any given situation. By creating the acceptable responses to a given situation, norms contribute to positive social outcomes for everyone. In contrast, when norms are broken and an unacceptable response is given, the person who broke the norms is more likely to experience disapproval from the larger social group.

Take for example, the idea that all children should be born within the confines of wedlock. While this is no longer a norm for much of American society, it has been a norm of many cultures and societies, including American society in years past, since the dawn of civilization. In many pre-modern societies, women were expected to remain a virgin until they were married. The point of this societal rule, or norm, wasn't really to prevent women from sexually enjoying their bodies, though some cultures and societies eventually adopted this attitude. The original purpose of the norm was so that the husband could ensure any offspring of the union were his. While this logic has a lot of flaws, society demanded virginal brides so a man didn't have to worry about his wife coming into their union pregnant with another man's child, thereby allowing illegitimate offspring to potentially inherit wealth that was not rightfully theirs.

If a woman broke this norm, she would be shunned by society and even the child would suffer the social stigma of being born a bastard, something he or she certainly had no control over. Even well into the 1950s and 60s, women who got pregnant outside of marriage would be sent to live in unwed mothers' homes, which were not inviting or welcoming in the least. Women would often be forced to give up their children for adoption or, in some cases, told their child had died shortly after birth in order to facilitate an illegal adoption. Centuries ago, both poor and wealthy mothers would often give their children to a paid baby farmer under the promise the mistress would care for or adopt the child, only for them to then be promptly murdered or left to die from neglect. Amelia Dyer was one such famous baby farmer, and the term eventually came to be one of derision.

Norms are generally implicit, but it's important to note they are extremely strong influences on the society they are operating within. Norms automatically create a set of responses that are supposed to enhance or provide protection to the group, while violating society's norms will lead to disapproval. Norms also have a different prominence in different cultures. For example, in collectivistic cultures one may witness cooperation in response to one another's needs (e.g., when you promise to love your spouse in sickness and in health) whereas in individualistic cultures one is more likely to witness cooperation through the norm of reciprocity (e.g., I'll let you live here rent-free, but only if you pay all the utilities).

Whether or not someone buys in to the concepts of cooperation or competition is often related to their beliefs and actual observations of other people's behaviors. In general, cooperation leads to more cooperation whereas competition leads to more competition. A person's beliefs regarding other people's willingness to cooperate and compete are strongly interwoven with that person's own willingness to cooperate or compete. In the context of relationships, there is a social-evolutionary basis for the functionality of the so-called tit-for-tat strategy. This strategy, which begins with a cooperative choice and subsequently imitates the other person's previous choice, is one of the most effective means for eliciting stable patterns of mutual cooperation. Indeed, tit-for-tat effectively rewards cooperation by acting cooperatively in response to cooperative actions. At the same time, tit-for-tat punishes competition by acting noncooperatively in response to competitive actions.

Competition

In the United Kingdom, there used to be a television gameshow called *Golden Balls*.

In the final round of the game, the contestants are given two golden balls each, one with the word "split" written on it and one with the word "steal" written on it. Per the rules of the game, the contestants have built up a jackpot of money thus far and now it has to be dispersed. If both contestants decide to split the money, they each get half the jackpot. If one contestant steals while the other splits, the stealing contestant gets the entire jackpot, and if both contestants steal, both contestants get nothing. This game has been quite interesting to social scientists, because why wouldn't every contestant just automatically choose to split? Getting half of something is far better than walking away empty-handed, right? Well, the reason that doesn't happen has a lot to do with competition.

The average person automatically assumes that others around them will compete, not cooperate.[xxxix] Because a lot of competition is perceived rather than something that actually takes place, it's good information for you to have in mind when you approach conflict resolution. When you can find solutions that are mutually beneficial to all parties, getting agreement or solving a key issue may not be the knock-down-drag-out fight you thought it was going to be. Hopefully, you'll be pleasantly surprised.

Competition is also not a bad thing at all. Scientifically, using a functional Near-Infrared Spectroscopy (fNIRS) helmet, scientists have been able to measure brain activity and see that competition can improve cognitive performance. This was seen when test subjects would increase their effort when their goals were in conflict with other test subjects'. Competition also increased self-perception by using subjective internal judgment, which increased cerebral responsiveness, and led to positive performance outcomes. These areas were previously inadequately unexplored in research. Another area that is not well researched explores how these areas are impacted by social context (e.g., cheering or booing). If a subject hears cheering or is told they are doing a good job, this reinforces their internal judgment, and their performance improves by running faster or increasing their output.[xl]

Results from studies regarding competition and brain response show that positive feedback leads to higher performance.[xli] This type of information is a gift for anyone who works to lead and guide others. Positive reinforcement produces more powerful results than negative consequences. Think about this in your role as boss, teacher, coach, parent, manager, leader, etc. If you understand your positive praise and feedback will take the person/people you are working with further than any kind of negative reinforcement such as castigation, yelling, or humiliation, you are on track to have your team performing at optimum performance rather than trudging along like a turtle swimming in peanut butter.

One thing to note about these studies, however, is that these are highly controlled studies conducted under a specific set of circumstances. In real life, people don't have this luxury. You, in no way, can predict the things that may be said to you or the behavior of a real opponent.[xlii] Some people are completely 100% on the up and up as a competitor, or they want you to do the best you can and support you in your career as your boss. Other supervisors may take out their anger and frustration on their subordinates, and if you're in that situation, I encourage you to get out of it as quickly as possible. Other kinds of opponents play dirty, bend the rules, or outright cheat. This is certainly different in cooperation. In cooperation, planned study or not, you and your group or partner are actively working together toward a common goal. You don't need to predict certain behaviors because you're already collaborating.

Cooperation and Competition

As I stated earlier in this chapter, cooperation and competition don't exist in a vacuum. They can exist together, and they each affect the brain in different ways. Neither cooperation nor competition is inherently good or inherently bad, as a lot of how well a person functions in a group or society is dependent on the rules of the unit. In the 2013 film, *The Wolf of Wall Street*, Jordan Belfort is enticed into a hedonistic lifestyle by being told a stockbroker's job is to make as much money as possible for himself. There are similar films about Wall Street, such as 1987's *Wall Street, Boiler Room* (2000), and also from 2000, *American Psycho,* which is based on the novel of the same name by Bret Easton Ellis. Christian Bale's portrayal of the psychotic Patrick Bateman in *American Psycho* takes the concept of competition and revs it up 100 times. All of these films thrive in the conflict of the intense twenty-four-hour competition that the protagonist nearly cracks under or comes into conflict with in one way or another. It can be said that stockbrokers perform a job that thrives on competition, and so they would need to enjoy and flourish in it as a major aspect of their life.

When I think about films that embody idea of cooperation, I can think of a few, like the movie *Toy Story* (1995). The theme song of the film is "You've Got a Friend in Me." Buzz and Woody have to work together to get back home or they will both be ripped apart by Sid, a kid who destroys toys, and left behind when Andy moves to the new house. Buzz and Woody may have started off as enemies, but by the end of the film, they have found a friend in each other. Other films that echo the cooperation theme include *Remember the Titans* (2000), the *Lord of the Rings* series (2001, 2002, 2003), and *Cool Runnings* (1993).

Despite the need for competition to exist, most of us get along just fine when we choose to, well, get along. Research has shown that cooperation is associated with a higher perceived membership in the group as well as higher self-efficacy, and it reinforces our perception we hold a high position within the social hierarchy of the unit. Cooperative attitudes were also shown to strengthen interpersonal attitudes. However, it should be noted that cooperation can lead to a poorer performance than a competitive one.[xliii] Now that you are aware of that, be extra careful regarding your performance and make sure you aren't letting yours slip with the expectation that someone else can pick up your slack. Whether you are intentionally thinking that or not, you don't want to fall into that trap.

Both cooperative and competitive attitudes require individuals to take on the perspectives of others, be empathetic, and the ability to adjust our behavior to the behavior of others. However, it's not cooperative but competitive scenarios when these subjective abilities are often present. That might seem odd because it would stand to reason that being empathetic and seeing things from another's perspective seem like cooperative skills. That's because they are. Remember that the difference between cooperation and competition is the end goal: finding a solution that benefits everyone vs. a solution that benefits oneself.

One area where cooperation is much more rewarding than competition is social interaction. Both the DLVPFC (the D in this abbreviation is dorsal) and VLPFC (refer back to Chapter 2) have been shown to be involved in ranking considerations when part of social interactions. The involvement of these areas of the brain, that implicate perception of social performance, correlate to high-level, top-down processes resultant from affective responses as it relates to social status.[xliv] This type of process within the brain helps you know what behaviors are and are not socially appropriate for any given situation and provide you with appropriate social motivation to be successful in a variety of social settings.

Research has shown that competitive behaviors are generally not rewarded in social interactions, and this consequently has a negative effect on social motivation. Additionally, recent research has suggested that motivations and emotions can influence our perception of positive or negative thoughts in relationships.[xlv] It's clear that both motivation and emotional components are a factor in social interactions and perceptions of social hierarchy. It's just not clear how much. Therefore, any actions that have a negative effect on social motivation will naturally have a negative impact on the feelings around social interactions.

Behavioral Activation System/Behavioral Inhibition System Research Study[xlvi]

In the BAS/BIS Research study conducted by Balconi, Crivelli, and Vanutelli (2017), the study consisted of twenty-two undergraduate students. Participants with known mental health issues or known mental health issues of immediate family members were excluded. State-Trait-Anxiety-Inventory (STAI) and the Beck Depression Inventory (BDI-II) were administered after the experimental session with no noted neurological or pathological concerns observed. The study was approved by the ethics committee of the Department of Psychology of The Catholic University of Milan.

Participants were brought to a fairly well-lit room and seated with a monitor screen about 25 inches from their face. Subjects were asked to complete a simple task on sustained selective attention and informed some measures about attentive performance would be used to evaluate personal skills to improve motivation. They were also told those skills would then be used to evaluate their teamwork skills and potential career success. Participants were also told that the task was a cooperative one as they were placed in pairs, though a black screen separated them. The participants were instructed the scoring would be based on their ability to produce synchronized responses with their partner in terms of accuracy and response time, but they were not permitted to communicate with their partner.

The participants were told to choose target stimuli among non-targets. The targets consisted of a four-combination geometric shape and color combination: triangle and circles, blue and green. Stimuli were displayed for .5 seconds with .3-second intervals in between. After each trial, constituted by three rounds of stimuli, the participants received a feedback of either a double arrows up, a high cooperation score; a dash, an average performance; or double down arrows, meaning a poor cooperation performance. These feedbacks were displayed for 5 seconds and were preceded and followed by eight blanks that were each 5 seconds as well. Each participant completed 200 trials.

Halfway through the trials, each participant was given a generalized evaluation of their overall performance and cooperation. As well, each partnership received a score of 89% on speed synchronicity and a score of 94% on accuracy synchronicity. Throughout the second half of the trials, 70% of cases received positive (double up arrows) or neutral (dash) feedback while 30% of the cases received negative (double down arrows). Participants were then asked to provide a self-evaluation of their performance using a seven-point Likert scale, where 1 = very low and 7 = very high. This questionnaire, in addition to a post-experiment questionnaire, showed that the majority (94%) were strongly engaged in the hierarchical scenario, 94% also stated to have a high level of trust in the feedback they had received and its accuracy, 97% felt strongly about the relevancy of the game for social status, and 92% of the participants perceived an upgrade in their social status while engaged in the study.

Behavioral Activation System (BAS) scores and Behavioral Inhibition System (BIS) scores were calculated for each participant. BAS scores used the Italian version of the Carver and White Questionnaire and a four-point Likert scale of twenty questions and four filler questions for a total of twenty-four questions. There were two scores garnered from this questionnaire, the BIS score—with a score range between 7-28 (7 items)—and the BAS score—with a score range between 13-52 (13 items). The questionnaire had items used to measure the following subsets of the BAS: drive (4 items), fun seeking (4 items), and reward (5 items). The average values are as follows:

BAS: 48.13
Drive: 13.88
Fun Seeking: 13.54
Reward: 23.7

The researchers did not disclose BIS scores for their research, stating that participants all had BIS scores lower than the BAS scores and that those scores were not used in this phase of the research. For our purposes, it's important to note that individuals with a high BAS score will be dominant in social interactions or have positive outcomes from their social interactions. Perhaps this person controls the topics of conversation, decides what stores are visited, or what restaurant is chosen to eat at. Maybe this person is the life of the party and always has a witty or funny joke at hand. In contrast, individuals with a high BIS score will traditionally be submissive or face negative consequences in social interactions. Maybe this is someone who feels insecure, so they boast overly loudly at the office holiday party, or this could be the proverbial henpecked husband, who is ruled by his controlling wife who browbeats his spirit down to specks of dust.

Chapter 4: Racism and Health

On Monday, December 21, 2015, Barbara Dawson, 57, was arrested at Liberty County Hospital in Blountstown, Florida. She was arrested for disorderly conduct and trespassing because she refused to leave the hospital. She was still in pain, she had said, and she was having trouble breathing. The officer who arrested her escorted her to his car where she promptly collapsed and was unresponsive. Barbara Dawson was readmitted to the hospital where she died from a blood clot in her lung an hour later.

A woman named Toshanna Ward, 25, died on January 2, 2020, when she was told she would have to wait two to six hours to see a doctor. She died after leaving the hospital and collapsing. She left to find help faster as she'd already waited over three hours. A chest X-ray revealed she had cardiomegaly, an enlarged heart, which had been the result of a stillborn pregnancy she'd had in March.

Both of these stories and many, many more are a result of what is called implicit bias in healthcare. Implicit bias theory was developed in the 1970s by Samuel Gaertner, Ph.D., from the University of Delaware and John F. Dovidio, Ph.D., from Yale University, both professors of psychology. Implicit bias theory states that people may hold negative unconscious feelings and beliefs about others based on their race or ethnicity that is different from their conscious attitudes.[19] So whether intentional or not, healthcare providers have the ability to let their subconscious thoughts and feelings override their personal aims and even professional ethics to treat everyone equally and without bias. We all do, but in healthcare settings, this is potentially fatal, and we'll be looking more into that in this chapter.

What is Racism, Its Structure, and Who Does it Affect?[xlvii][xlviii]

Racism is a set of behaviors, intentional or not, that result in unfair and avoidable inequalities in power, resources, and opportunities across racial and ethnic groups. It can be expressed in stereotypes, discrimination, microaggressions, prejudices, and beliefs, and can range from direct threats or insults to systems that are deeply ingrained in social systems and structures.

Racism isn't something that is just person to person. It can occur at multiple levels. It can be internal. There are actually two types of internalized racism. The first is internalized dominance, which is when someone views their racial group as superior in comparison to others. This might be someone who joins a White nationalist group. In contrast, internalized oppression is when a person views their racial group as inferior to others. This may be someone of Hispanic or Latino descent, particularly as the United States has made more aggressive moves regarding illegal immigration, sanctuary cities, and deportation of illegal immigrants who may have been in the country since childhood.

Racism can also be interpersonal, in other words, interactions between people. This might be something like when a person of color uses food stamp benefits to pay for items at the grocery store, and in response the cashier rolls their eyes and makes a snide comment about "you people" always being on the government payroll. Of course, no one is privy to the reason why this person is receiving food benefits. It could be due to recent job loss, taking in foster children, adoption of a child. It's none of our business. Additionally, racism can be systemic, which consists of the production, control, and access to things based on race or ethnicity such as work, housing, and other resources, or symbolic materials in society. This could look like the inability to secure a stable job with benefits, which then has an effect on the ability to secure stable housing, reliable transportation, and affordable healthcare, as healthcare benefits are often tied to employment in the United States.

When one or more groups are systematically oppressed for any reason, other groups—in the case of race, Whites—receive an unearned advantage. This is what is meant when we talk about the word privilege, which can come in many forms based on age or social class or sex. Experiencing these oppressions drive health and well-being, and what people experience when they receive healthcare is directly related to race, among other factors.

Racism as a Determinant of Health[xlix]

The effect of racism on health has predominantly focused on how it affects health via several recognized pathways, many of which we mentioned before. The effect that racism has on health can lead to the inability to secure stable housing, stable employment, education, and brings more exposure to risk factors such as racial violence, gang violence, and crime. Studies have also focused on the negative mental health outcomes people experience as a result of racism such as hypervigilance, anticipatory or attributional anxiety, and continual thinking on sad or dark thoughts, which is called rumination.

Individuals who experience racism will also experience more wear and tear on their bodies and be more susceptible to disease due to experiencing chronic stress and a high neuroendocrine response from that stress over time. Individuals are also less likely to choose to engage in adaptive activities such as eating right and exercise. This can be for a variety of reasons such as lack of time or money or access. Similarly, they may choose to engage in unhealthy behaviors like drinking alcohol or smoking, either as a way to self-medicate or as a means to cope with stress. And finally, research has been done on racism and how it leads to individuals becoming victims of race-related violence.

One of the biggest challenges of researching the effects of racism is attributing any one action or consequence directly to racism. In controlled laboratory studies, it's truly only possible to determine the probability that the results are due to racism and not other factors. Bearing the difficulties of measuring the effects of racism in mind, there are two ways racism and healthcare research is conducted: by indirect inference and direct experience.

When researchers utilize the indirect approach, they essentially remove other possibilities from the list of possible causes of the test subject's experience. They will take a list of variables—was the patient a woman, low income, insured, racially or ethnically diverse, etc., and tick them off one after the other until race and ethnicity are the probable culprits. This is done by making causal connections to draw conclusions about the actions that occurred as well as through a process called decomposition, which is breaking down complicated problems into simpler components.

Direct experience is given by the test subject via direct or self-report. When it comes to the self-report, there are some factors that have to be considered. These are overestimation, underestimation, and cognitive/affective and methodological factors. Overestimation may happen when a person feels a need to blame others for their experience or parts of their identity are entwined with seeing racism in every action. Think of this as someone who may be heavily involved with the New Black Panther Party, which is a designated hate group by both the Anti-Defamation League and the Southern Poverty Law Center. This particular group was only chosen as an example as members *may* feel as if they have a point to prove. Please note this group is not affiliated with the Black Panther Party.

In contrast, underestimation may be caused by norms or societal pressures and internalized racism that somewhat blinds a person to the racism occurring to or around them. Think of this as a person who is told they speak "White" rather than with a dialect or slang common to specific races, such as Ebonics. Issues with the cognitive/affective and methodological areas of a study can include using racially charged language or using language that indicates there is a social desirability bias that can increase or decrease the perception and reporting of racism.

Reactions and responses to racism affect health in different ways, depending on how the individual reacts. Individuals may respond cognitively, behaviorally, or emotionally. They may also have a passive response or one that is active. The response may also be adaptive or maladaptive.

Blaming "the man" for your inability to find a good and steady job despite your qualifications and education would be a cognitive, active, maladaptive response to the difficulties of finding a job, which can be difficult for anybody to endure. A more productive response, a behavioral, active, adaptive response, might be calling and contacting all your friends and contacts to inquire about any openings they know about and putting it out there you are looking for a job in your field. Taking that action might help land you a few interviews, at the very least.

I'll be the first to tell you blame is my favorite coping mechanism, but I say it in jest. Blame doesn't achieve anything, solve anything, and it's a bit like drinking poison and expecting someone else to die. You just fester on the inside and become angry and bitter at whoever it is you're blaming for your trouble, rather than seeking out real solutions to your problems.

Emotional responses to racism can be directed inward or outward. These can also be active or passive, and outward-directed emotional responses, which are by definition active, can also be empowered or disempowered. Inward-directed emotional responses that are active might include feeling self-loathing, shame, or anxiety, while passive inward responses include depression, hopelessness, and confusion. Outward responses to racism that are empowered might be exuding a feeling of amusement, contempt, or sympathy for the person displaying racist attitudes or beliefs, while disempowered responses would involve feelings of rage, hate, and frustration.

It is undeniable that some of the biggest impacts of racism on health occur at an organizational level. Scientists and researchers have debated whether or not a nonhuman entity can even have such an influence, let alone such a deeply impactful one, on the human condition. One way we can show beyond a doubt that organizations do possess the mechanisms to be racist is via residential racial segregation. In both historical and modern times, in societies of numerous races, the dominant race could restrict the areas in which nondominant races could live. This occurred and was legal in the United States until Congress passed the Fair Housing Act in 1968. That's only fifty-two years ago, not even two generations. Depending on your age, your parents might remember not being able to live in a certain area of town or choosing to live in an area of town because others could not, and that was considered desirable in that day and age. It's crazy to think about how far we've come in fifty-two years and yet realize it's not nearly far enough.

Residential segregation still happens today, but it is based more on the economics of the cost of living as well as what landlords accept subsidized housing benefits. Also, when certain areas become revitalized through gentrification, this often causes rent increases in the area to rise drastically, and this in turn prices lower income people out of the market, pushing them out of these newly reinvigorated parts of the community. While gentrification is not targeted at any specific race, it is targeted at the socioeconomically disadvantaged, and these people are more likely to be minorities.

Residential segregation has a number of negative impacts on health. It leads to a higher mortality rate for both infants and adults as well as disparities in the treatment of certain chronic and infectious diseases. Residential segregation also harms health by decreasing access to high-quality nutritious foods, either by access or cost; access to usable and maintained recreational facilities and equipment; and exposure to crime as well as toxic substances in the environment like pollution or waste—such as when Ford Motor Company dumped toxic paint sludge onto land belonging to the Ramapough Mountain Indian Tribe, causing illness and disease in nearly every family in the community.

Unilaterally, researchers on racism and health have found a strong link between racism and both physical and mental health. In fact, in a meta-analysis of 293 research articles on this topic, the relationship was strongest for poor mental health and weaker for physical health. Mental health is about twice as strongly related to racism as physical health. Mental health issues included diagnoses like depression and anxiety. While the meta-analysis did not find a link between high blood pressure, there is a clear link between weight gain and obesity, which can cause high blood pressure in the future or if the weight gain is accompanied by a diet high in fatty and fried foods. There is also strong evidence to suggest that maladaptive behaviors such as illicit drug use, alcohol use, and smoking are all strongly tied to racist experiences.

It's unclear exactly why the link between racism and poor mental health is so strong. It could be that the nature of self-reporting responses used by many studies could lead to some overestimation or biases in the responses. It's also possible that the weaker relationship between physical health and racism is due, in part, to the fact that some health factors take time to set in or act "invisibly" in the body unbeknownst to the individual. This can include illnesses like high blood pressure, type 2 diabetes, thyroid problems, sleep apnea, coronary artery disease, fatty liver disease, and any number of hidden health issues you may not even be aware are killing you. Whether or not it's intentional, being passive or avoiding addressing a health condition doesn't make it go away. It makes it worse.

A few months ago, I got a sharp shooting pain on the lower left side of my mouth. I figured I had a sensitive tooth, so I drank from a straw for a few days and brushed with some toothpaste made for people with sensitive teeth. Everything seemed great and I just went on my merry way. Then I went out of town on a business trip. Something must have happened while I was flying through the air at 30,000 feet, because by the next morning the pain I had been experiencing a few months before was coming in intermittent waves and getting worse. I called my dentist from the hotel and was able to get in the following morning at 10 a.m. I took some prescription-strength anti-inflammatories and used an ice pack the second I walked in the door at home to make it to my appointment. Yep, that tooth I thought was just sensitive was brewing with infection, and now it had to come out or be root canaled. Neither option was a particularly positive one for me. I had ignored the problem months prior and, instead of maybe filling a cavity, I needed to have a molar removed, which was no easy feat since no one in my town would touch the job without sedating me, which I am probably grateful for.

It took me over a week to figure out what I was going to do. Part of the reason is that even with dental insurance the cost for either procedure was over $1000, which is a lot of money to just plop down on the counter. Imagine trying to come up with that kind of money when you don't know where your rent is going to come from or your next meal. When your basic needs aren't met, things like health care and certainly mental health care will be seen as extravagant extras that can't be afforded. It's a terrible thing to think about, to imagine needing therapy or medication for depression or anxiety and not being able to get it due to racism—any reason really, but certainly one as avoidable as racism.

How to fight racism using critical thinking?

Several experts shared their thoughts and observations about how best to deal with racism through evidence-based strategies. Carol Tavris said, "racism and prejudice are thorny, age-old problems with many origins. There is no single solution, no magic spell that will bring everyone together. But—like any human endeavor—some evidence-based approaches show more promise than others." Stephen Pinker and Michael Shermer elaborate in their books *The Better Angels of Our Nature and The Moral Arc*, that historical trends for humanity are encouraging. We are headed toward a more cooperative world.

Research-based evidence suggests that racial biases can be diminished using personal engagement instead of hostile reactions. Calling people racist isn't going to make anyone less racist. The most ineffective way to deal with racism is to attack or insult them. Why? Because the only thing we'd accomplish is just fueling their narrative of victimhood and getting them sympathy— maybe even from people who otherwise disagree with their views.[1]

When trying to challenge someone's racist world view it's a good start to have your end goal in mind, namely to help that person be less prejudiced and judgmental about a certain race. As we know by now, telling them that they are wrong and they should change is not an approach that will facilitate our end goal. As hard as it is, try to think with their heads. If you had a racist conviction and people told you that you were wrong, would you be like "yes, I guess I had a mistaken world view all my life, thanks for letting me know?" Probably not. You'd become defensive, clam up, and have even more hostile feelings. A better approach is to think about "what could someone tell me or show me that would change my mind about a deeply held belief?" It would probably be something empirical, something real that actively disproves my narrative. For racists, in this case, would be meeting, talking, interacting, befriending someone from the group they dislike. The unknown is always scary. Once we get familiar with something –or someone- our brain will create new memories and programs saying, "oh, this is not dangerous." Optimally, the path of familiarity and empirical exposure will lead the person whose view we want to change in the right direction.

It's crucial to use critical thinking when coming up with solutions to find racism because the natural, sensible gut reaction, "stop that, don't be racist" won't help us reach our goal.

Chapter 5: Ingroup versus Outgroup

Social Identity Theory

Henri Tajfel was a Polish Jew who moved to France to study chemistry at the Sorbonne because he wasn't permitted into university under the Nazi regime. When World War II broke out, he fought on the side of the French, but was captured as a German POW. He was uncertain if he should disclose his status as a Jew. Though he readily admitted he was a French citizen, he never denied being Jewish. After the war, Henri returned home to discover the vast majority of his friends and family had perished in the Holocaust and, like many survivors, this had a profound effect on him. His experiences as he'd watched Hitler come to power and then what happened to "other" Jews, Gypsies, homosexuals, and the disabled were what eventually led him to his study in psychology and intergroup relations.[li]

109

Under Tajfel's theory, he suggested that the groups we belong to, such as our family, religious organizations, and work groups, are all an important source of our pride and self-esteem. Being a member of these groups gives us a sense of identity and belonging, and that is extremely powerful. In our minds, we compartmentalize ourselves into groups of "us" and "them," and one of the ways we do this is through our membership in these social groups.[lii]

Tajfel's theory states that in order to facilitate putting ourselves into these groups, we tend to exaggerate the similarities within the group in order to create what is called the ingroup. Members of the group also look to exaggerate the differences of individuals who are not in the group, and these people are called the outgroup. The main hypothesis of Tajfel's theory is that members of the ingroup work to find negative aspects of members of the outgroup in order to enhance their self-image.[liii]

Think back to the running theme of team sports. If you have a favorite team, that team probably has a rival that they despise and try to win against more than any other team; this is particularly so in college football. Some of the great rivalries in college football are between Ohio State University and the University of Michigan, the University of Alabama and Auburn University, Army and Navy, and the University of Texas and the University of Oklahoma. Depending on which team you support, you are either an ingroup or outgroup (you are both simultaneously). However, in the days leading up to the game, there tends to be a lot of trash-talking by the coaches, the players, and the fans of each team. The coach from the University of Alabama may say that the quarterback from Auburn only knows how to throw interceptions, or a University of Michigan defensive lineman might tell an offensive player from Ohio State he'll mow him down on the field. The point of the trash talk is to boost the egos of the players and coaches in your ingroup so they will be pumped for the big game.

Social identity theory proposes that there is a three-step mental process to reaching the "us versus them" mentality. These stages are social categorization, social identification, and social comparison.[liv]

Social Categorization:[lv] Social categorization is when we break down things, or in this case, people, into categories so we can identify them. Some categories can include Hispanic, male, Muslim, nurse, teacher. All of these categories assign some kind of social role to the person you are categorizing. Additionally, by knowing what our ingroups are, we know what norms shape our behavior.

Social Identification:[lvi] In this stage, we adopt the behaviors of our ingroup. For example, as a teacher, I have a very strict code of ethics, and simply drinking alcoholic beverages in public can get me into trouble, especially if I were to appear to be intoxicated. Because such an activity could cause me to lose my teaching certificate, I do not drink in public. It's important to note that belonging to your ingroups has significant meaning to you as a person, and your self-esteem is heavily interwoven into your status within the group.

Social Comparison:[lvii] This is the final stage of the social identity theory. Now that you have joined a group and adopted their behaviors, you now have to identify competing groups or rivals. This will create the "us versus them" mentality, as you compete not only for resources but also for your self-image.

Case Study: A Class Divided[lviii]

One of the most impactful experiments on ingroups and outgroups was not conducted in a controlled laboratory setting or by a psychologist. It was conducted in an elementary school classroom by third grade teacher Jane Elliot. The day after Martin Luther King, Jr. was assassinated on April 4, 1968, Ms. Elliot divided her class into two groups. The ingroup consisted of the blue-eyed students and the outgroup was comprised of all the brown-eyed students. In a matter of moments the blue-eyed seven-year-olds were shunning their peers, ridiculing and calling them names. They ignored their classmates on the playground during recess and called them stupid. Ms. Elliott then switched the circumstances and the blue-eyed children became the outgroup while the brown-eyed children became the ingroup. Rather than having learned what it felt like to be treated so poorly, the brown-eyed children immediately began treating their peers in the same manner in which they had been treated.

It's clear that the sense of belonging to a group, particularly the group in power, carries a significant amount of psychological power for us. There have been many studies, such as Milgram's shock study, that show how easily influenced humans can be. Real-life consequences of this mob-like mentality have included the Holocaust, the Rwandan Genocide, and the Bosnian Genocide with tragic consequences. Understanding how and why this occurs is one thing social scientists continue to try to comprehend.

The Neuroscience Behind Ingroups and Outgroups

Imagine you have been selected to serve as a juror on a civil injury lawsuit. The plaintiff is suing a company whose truck driver ran a red light and caused an accident, resulting in the plaintiff losing his left arm. As part of the evidence, the plaintiff's attorney introduces photographs of the plaintiff in the hospital just after surgery where he is grimacing in pain. He clearly is uncomfortable, and his medical reports show a level of depression and despondency associated with the sudden loss of his limb. The plaintiff's recovery was difficult. He got an infection in the hospital, and he's had months of rehab to learn how to live his life without two arms. The plaintiff is suing the trucking company for three million dollars. The defendant readily agrees they are at fault for the accident, but argues the plaintiff's demands are unreasonable. His arm isn't worth three million dollars, so they are trying the case in the hope of a reduced award. As a juror, what would you do?

Neuroimaging has shown that seeing another person in pain activates the parts of our own brain that is responsible for pain. However, this mirroring of the neural response is not constant. It is tempered by our beliefs, such as if the person in pain acted fairly or unfairly. If the person is in pain because they were shot holding up a liquor store, then we are less likely to feel as much empathy for their pain. On the other hand, the plaintiff in the example above, who did nothing wrong, will cause others to have a stronger neurological response. However, the issue that the trucking company brings up, the three-million-dollar payout, could lead to a diminished neural response similar to that of the person who was shot holding up the liquor store, as financial transactions tend to lower our pain response neurologically.[lix]

Additionally, research has shown that when it comes to interpersonal interactions, positive feedback and knowing that one's own performance impacts another's positively impacts performance and output. The test subject will also change their performance level depending on whether their actions are competitive, cooperative, neither, or cause pain to their partner. Have you ever been giving a presentation and your boss walks in, so you straighten your posture, give a big smile, and project confidence as you finish out the presentation? According to activity in the ventral striatum, just simply being watched improves our performance.[lx]

We already know that being observed within an ingroup does positively impact our behavior. One area we want to look further into is whether or not it matters who in the ingroup is doing the observation. One study has found that the mPFC is activated when individuals connect even tenuously with groups. These are often very broad social categorizations, and brain activity and neural pathways when observing ingroup members versus outgroup members have shown to display broad discriminatory attitudes and views.[lxi]

It has been hypothesized that if the ingroup in question is tied in the slightest way to a test subject's identity, they will connect to the group, causing the initiation of brain activity that is far different than when the test subject associates a group as an outgroup. These differences in brain activity would show the different levels of motivation depending on a participant's level of belonging.[lxii] Researchers have shown that there is a much stronger reaction to prosocial action on behalf of ingroups such as sports teams or racial groups. Generally, these prosocial actions can allow for the prediction of behavior in everything from jury selection to profiling to genocide.[lxiii] This type of behavior is one way we are able to predict the outcome of elections.

Case Study: Neural Responses to Predict Group Allegiance[lxiv]

In this study, the researchers ran three experiments. Experiment one was a study of ingroup versus outgroup, experiment two was a study of flexibility, and the third experiment measured arbitrary teams. The researchers recruited 135 participants, though thirty were later excluded due to issues related to brain imaging. Of the 105 remaining participants, sixty-seven were used in experiment one with a subset of fourteen used in experiment two. Fourteen separate subjects were used in experiment three. Of note, twenty-four participants were excluded from experiment two on the basis of their self-identification of being agnostic. This study was classified as deceptive as the true nature of the study was not disclosed to test subjects.

In preparation for the experimental phase of the study, the researchers had identified regions in the brain associated with pain-related empathy by using blood-oxygenated-level-dependent (BOLD) imaging and fMRI. Participants were alternately show videos of a hand being stabbed by a needle or stroked by a cotton swab to view which areas of the brain were activated.

Experiment 1: Ingroup vs. Outgroup – In this experiment, there were six different hands for subjects to view and they were all labeled with a different religious group: Christian, Jew, Hindu, Muslim, Scientologist, and Atheist. Participants were randomly assigned to one of six groups for the study and stayed in that group for its duration. Results showed that once in their ingroups, when the participants viewed their groups' hands being touched, their empathy reactions were much strong than it was for that of their outgroups.

Experiment 2: Flexibility – In this study, the researchers attempted to tie former religious outgroup members to an ingroup through the use of an alliance. Participants were randomly assigned to two groups of three hands. The green team consisted of the Muslims, Jews, and Atheists, while the blue team was comprised of the Christians, Scientologists, and Hindus. The participants then received a textbox that three of the religions were now at war with the other three. The outgroup religions that were not on the same team together were considered to be allies. One of the outcomes of this experiments was that according to the self-reports from the participants, the classifier of strength in religious beliefs was strongly correlated with prediction confidence, meaning the strength of ingroup affiliation is likely dependent on certainty in the ingroups.

Experiment 3: Arbitrary Teams – Participants were randomly assigned to one of two fictional groups, the Justinians or Augustinians, by flipping a coin. Each person was then given a corresponding bracelet to wear indicating their team affiliation. The intent of the bracelet was to serve as a reminder of the participant's team as well as help create a bond to that team. From here, the experiment ran the same as in experiment one.

Behaviorally, the participants had been told they were watching the hands being stabbed to see how pain affected memory, and the researchers bolstered this claim by providing feedback and "scoring" the performance on 20% of the trials at random in order to improve alertness. However, the primary result was that the arbitrary ingroup discriminated against the arbitrary outgroup, which resulted in a 70% area under the curve (AUC). With an AUC this high, there is a good indication the researchers' model is able to distinguish between classes.

Case Study: Ingroup Disadvantages in Recognizing Microexpressions[lxv]

Eighty-four Chinese undergraduate students participated in this experiment. Researchers pulled a set of facial expressions from the BU-3DFE database, which contains images of over 100 models from different ethnic and racial backgrounds and microexpressions. The age ranges of the models range from ten to seventy years of age. Each model poses for seven different facial expressions: happy, sad, fear, surprise, disgust, anger, and neutral. For the purposes of this study, the researchers excluded the neutral expression. The intensity of the expressions also come in four levels: low, middle, high, and very high. The researchers selected to use only the "very high" intensity expressions. This study used a combination of only White and Asian models for the identification of microexpressions. In this study, images of the Asian models were members of the ingroup while images of the White models served as members of the outgroup. All images were converted to grayscale and normalized to the average global mean.

Interestingly, this study found there was no ingroup advantage to identifying the microexpressions of the Asian models. In fact, being a member of the ingroup was a disadvantage, and the disadvantage wasn't mitigated by the microexpression test researchers had the participants take in order to help them more readily identify microexpressions. This was not an issue of skin color, as the photos had all been set to grayscale. This is also not a phenomenon unique to the Chinese. This lack of ingroup advantage has been reported of other Western cultures in similar studies. The Chinese participants are consistently unstable.

It's possible this is an issue that relates back to the competition versus cooperation issue where individuals engaged in cooperation perform at lower levels than those engaged in competition. If there is no motivation to accurately complete the trials, a lower performance level would lead to these types of outcomes. Another possibility might be that because we are already members of the ingroup, we spend more time analyzing the outgroup for weaknesses in the interest of our self-image, paying less attention to the traits of the ingroup.

Chapter 6: Social Influence

What is Social Influence?[lxvi]

In the episode "Raisins" from the television show *South Park* Stan decides to leave his regular group of friends and join up with the goth kids. In addition to each of the kids having their own list of woes, they are desperate not to become a "conformist." However, in the hilarity of the episode, they have managed to miss that, as much as they have tried not to, they are in fact conforming to a particular aesthetic—the goth aesthetic. When Stan asks how he joins the group of goth kids, he's told all he has to do is dress like them and listen to the same music they do, the requirement of conformity by the nonconformists flying right over everyone's heads.

While *South Park* is just a crude cartoon for adults, it often uses satire to point out particular points of view on many things happening in society today. It's a cartoon that both uses and has social influence. Social influence describes how our thoughts and feelings and behavior respond to the social world. This includes our tendencies to obey authority figures—this is why we don't argue with the police officer when we get pulled over for speeding when we know we were not; to conform to others; and to follow the rules of society. Social influence comes in two forms: implicit expectations and explicit expectations.

Implicit expectations are the unwritten rules of society or your social group, the norms you live by. These would be things like not picking your nose, not going to work without wearing makeup (for women in certain areas of the country), and not fighting with your spouse in public. These are actions and behaviors that would not be considered acceptable and would be frowned upon by others. Implicit expectation can then be further divided into two subsets: conformity and expectations from social roles.

Conformity is a set of behaviors you choose to adopt on your own. In the *South Park* example from above, Stan asks how to join the group of goth kids. He wants to know how to fit in with that crowd. When you were in high school, you probably did some level of conforming yourself. Depending on your age, maybe you had hair that was teased up as high as it would go and you were very knowledgeable about acid-wash denim. Perhaps you wore a lot of flannel, had a chain hooked to your wallet, and appeared as if you forgot to shower for a week. The point is that you did things to fit in with your peers—to a certain degree you probably still do—and this is what is known as conformity.

The other type of implicit expectation is set by the social roles we take on. There's a certain look and attitude we expect from "soccer moms." Generally, the soccer mom drives a minivan, has a short over-processed haircut, and shuffles her kids to and from a list of endless activities. As a high-powered businessman, you are expected to wear a suit, be rigid, have high expectations for your underlings, be demanding, drive an expensive car, etc. These are just, in many ways, stereotypical expectations we have for figures who hold these roles.

On the other hand, explicit expectations are clearly stated. These are laws, policies, and requirements. The two types of explicit expectations are compliance and obedience. Compliance is when you engage in a particular activity based on a request. If I ask you to move so I can get by, you most certainly will, but you don't have to. I don't have authority over you, and I can't punish you, but most people will move out of the way when asked to do so politely. In contrast, obedience is when you respond to a demand from some higher authority figure. If your boss walks into your office and drops a pile of data and work on your desk and says, "I want this on my desk by Friday," you know you better have that on his desk by Friday or else face the consequences of castigation or possibly losing your job.

Mass Psychogenic Illness[lxvii]

About 15 minutes after arriving at work, a Warren County High School teacher in Warren County, Tennessee, smelled a gasoline-like odor in her classroom. She soon developed a headache, nausea, dizziness, and shortness of breath, and so a mass psychogenic illness was triggered. A mass psychogenic illness occurs when individuals experience physical symptoms of illness, like the aforementioned headache and nausea, when there is no physical cause. As a result of the teacher's symptoms, the high school was evacuated and eighty students and nineteen teachers went to the emergency room, which resulted in thirty-eight of them being admitted.

The school then reopened after five days, and seventy-one more people went to the emergency room—but despite extensive testing, investigators could find no cause for any of the symptoms reported. Eventually, researchers noticed that these "illnesses" only occurred when they were in the line of sight of another "sick" person. Rashes were caused by scratching, not exposure to toxic substances; seeing someone you knew and believed was sick could cause the hyperventilation; and all the other symptoms were believed to be psychological, relating to conformity.

This case is incredibly fascinating because so many people experienced the mass psychological response. It's more than possible the first teacher smelled something odd and then developed these symptoms due to a migraine or some other neurological issue, but nearly 200 people in a rural community all getting a migraine in this fashion would be unheard of. The mass "outbreak" was likely one of fear, and the mass illness was something akin to the opposite of the placebo effect—when a patient feels better after receiving a placebo, but thinks they are receiving medication. Though not mentioned previously, the amygdala is the part of our brain responsible for processing fear. Universally, the study of how the brain processes fear, especially sustained fear (anxiety), has not been sufficiently researched and should be an area researchers look to investigate more thoroughly. Studying the brain is a very delicate and challenging process, as we rely exclusively on external forms of measurement.

The Stanford Prison Experiment

The Stanford Prison Experiment, conducted by Dr. Phil Zimbardo in 1971, is one of the most groundbreaking psychological experiments ever conducted, and nothing like it will ever be conducted again. One of the reasons for this is due to numerous ethical criticisms of Zimbardo and his methods. The American Psychological Association (APA) has now set a standard of ethics psychologists are sworn to uphold when conducting experiments. However, the lack of ethical guidelines is part of what makes this study and what it reveals about human behavior so impactful. Due to the controversial methods and the potential harm to the mental and physical health of the participants, it is highly doubtful a similar study would ever by approved by any university's Institutional Review Board.

The experiment involved twenty-for participants who were randomly assigned the role of either prisoner or prison guard, and two participants were left in reserve in case anyone dropped out. There were ten prisoners and eleven guards, one drop out, and two reserves.[29] Participants were paid $15 per day for their time. The experiment started with the "prisoners" being arrested at their homes and being taken, blindfolded, to the converted basement of the psychology building on the Stanford University campus. The prisoners were fingerprinted, had their mugshot taken, and booked into the prison.[lxviii] This began the process of deidentification.

Once arrived, the prisoners were told to undress completely. At this time, they were deloused, had any personal possessions taken from them, and provided with a uniform and a prisoner number. Henceforth prisoners were no longer referred to by name but by their prisoner number exclusively. The prison uniform consisted of a white smock with the prisoner's number, a nylon cap to cover their heads, and a locked chain around one ankle. Prisoners were not permitted any undergarments. Guards were also dressed in identical khaki uniforms and given a whistle and nightstick.[lxix]

Throughout the duration of the experiment, three guards worked a rotation of eight hours each, with others on call. Guards were given carte blanche to do what they felt they needed to do to maintain "law and order" in the prison, but they were not permitted to use physical violence. Originally, Zimbardo observed the behavior of the participants as a researcher, but later he became the prison warden.[lxx]

This experiment took place over six days in August 1971. The study was designed to see if situational pressures could overwhelm an individual's inherent personality, and within six days, the prison devolved into controlled chaos.

One of the things Zimbardo used in his study to create pressure and overwhelm the test subjects was deidentification. Deidentification is when a person's self-awareness disappears into the identity of the group or a social role.[lxxi] In this case, the role of prisoner or prison guard.

The role of the guard: The role of the guard is unique in this experiment because the guards were not required to stay in the prison around the clock. They were allowed to return home when they were not working their shifts, yet being away from the prison didn't change their behaviors inside the prison.[28] The symbols of the guards' uniforms and their nightsticks served as a reminder of their authority and spoke to their membership in the ingroup.[lxxii] This allowed them to deidentify themselves from their actions in order to carry out their behaviors.

The role of the prisoners: The deidentification process started immediately with the prisoners when they became nameless numbers. The symbol of carrying a chain around their ankle gave away their status that they were bound to the prison.[lxxiii]

Because of this extreme power differential and deidentification, which allowed the guards to excuse their actions as actions of the group and ignore their victims as individuals, brutality quickly overran the prison. One prisoner was forced to simulate a sex act, and one prisoner was taken to the "hole," a tiny supply closet, where other prisoners were instructed to bang on the door and berate him. One of the most fascinating aspects of this experiment is that no one instructed the participants on how to act. Both the prisoners and prison guards adopted their behavior based on their ideas of the social role they had been assigned.[lxxiv]

It is frightening how quickly humans can alter their behavior to fit whatever paradigm they need it to. But it's not altogether shocking either, as we've seen it before in other circumstances. The German people during the rise of the Third Reich easily fell under the power and charisma of Adolf Hitler and adopted many of this twisted views against other groups of people he found

135

to be undesirable. Their denial was so fierce, many Germans claimed they had no idea what was going on in death camps across Europe, despite some of the most prolific camps being located in Germany. During the Nuremburg trials, the defense offered up by many individuals was simply that they were just following orders. It is also well documented that some Jews even collaborated with the Nazis in exchange for more freedom or better treatment. Chaim Rumkowski is one of the most despicable of these collaborators, as he would submit the names of his rivals for deportation.

Milgram's Shock Experiments

In Milgram's shock experiments, three people took part in each trial of the study: the experimenter, the person conducting the study; the learner, who was an actor aware of the nature of the study; and the teacher, who was the actual subject of the study. When conducting each trial, the learner and the teacher arrived together, and were then escorted to a room where the learner was strapped into what appeared to be an electric chair "so he wouldn't escape." In later versions of Milgram's experiment, the learner would plead not to be left and state he had a heart condition.[lxxv]

Then the teacher would be taken to another room adjacent to the learner, where he would receive a shock to feel firsthand the "shock" the learner would receive each time the teacher responded with an incorrect answer. The experimenter would then show the teacher a series of cards with word pairs and then hold up a single word and ask the teacher to identify the pair. If the teacher was wrong, the learner received a shock. With each incorrect answer, the voltage of the fake shocks increased, and the learner played prerecorded responses expressing his increasing discomfort at each shock. When the learner was to receive the highest shock levels, they fell silent and did not respond.[lxxvi]

If at any time the teacher wanted to quit the experiment, the experimenter responded with oral prompts encouraging the teacher to continue the experiment, each more strongly worded than the last. If the teacher received all four prompts and still wanted to quit, then the experiment ended. It was also ended when the learned received three successive shocks of 450 volts three times in a row. In the event the teacher became concerned about the well-being of the learner, the teacher was told the learner would experience no permanent effects from participating in the experiment.[lxxvii]

Milgram ran this study eighteen times, and each time the results were the same. People were willing to cause pain and perhaps even death to a complete stranger simply because someone had instructed them to do it. When Milgram conducted trials with only women, the results didn't differ, either. Women were just as likely as men to inflict the same types of injuries to strangers who were completely innocent of any wrongdoing. One thing that did seem to cause the participants to hesitate was the presence of the learner in the same room where the experiment was taking place. The obedience level of the participants decreased even further when the teacher was required to place the learner's hand on a metal plate in order for the learner to receive the electric shock.[lxxviii]

Milgram's experiment shows how easily we are willing to obey the commands of a perceived authority figure. In 1974, members of the Peoples Temple, led by Jim Jones, moved to Guyana to start an agricultural commune. Setting up the commune was grueling. There was no running water, no electricity, no restroom facilities, and everything had to be built from the ground up. One of the tactics Jim Jones used to maintain control and obedience of this followers in Guyana would be to have them drink Kool-Aid he told them was laced with poison on occasions called "white nights." During these times, Jones would tell members of the temple genocide was happening in the streets, and he instructed them to drink cyanide-laced Kool-Aid to save themselves only for it to turn out none of what he said was true and the Kool-Aid was not poison at all.

Later, in 1978, the "white nights" turned out to be practice runs for a mass suicide conducted at Jonestown. 909 people died as a result of drinking poisoned Flavor Aid. It would have only taken minutes for the first effects of the cyanide that had been added to the drink to become apparent in the people who had taken the first few cups. However, Jim Jones's authority and hold on the temple members was so strong, they obeyed his authority to the point they killed themselves for him, and they had to have known that was going to happen as they watched others die in the jungle after having drunk the grape-flavored drink. Members of the Peoples Temple at Jonestown paid the ultimate price for their unwavering obedience to their leader.

Social Influence Theory

The crux of social influence theory is that a person's attitudes and beliefs, accompanied by their subsequent actions and behaviors, influences others. In Dr. Herbert Kelman's research he identifies three processes of social influence: compliance, identification, and internalization. These process can occur at different levels, which is attributed to how intensely an individual is willing to accept influence from others.[lxxix]

Compliance: Compliance occurs when an individual adopts specific behaviors in an effort to fit in or avoid punishment. Compliance is why you don't speed, at least not excessively, when you're driving. You don't want to have to pay for a speeding ticket or get points on your driver's license, which can make your insurance go up.[lxxx]

Identification: Identification is when you adopt or maintain certain behaviors in order to keep your membership in a group.[lxxxi] Identification is why you wear professional attire to work and behave in a professionally appropriate manner. You actually receive satisfaction from conforming to the standards set by the ingroup.

Internalization: Internalization occurs when you accept new behavior after perceiving it as being rewarding. You may also realize the new behavior aligns with your value system, and that makes the behavior attractive to you. It is the content of the new behavior that you find satisfactory. An example of internalization is joining a religious organization in a community that's heavily entwined with religious beliefs. You would receive community support as a reward, but if you are religious the beliefs of the organization would align with your own.[lxxxii]

Additional types of social influence include conformity, minority influence, reactance, obedience, psychological manipulation, abusive power and control, propaganda, and hard power. We will go over each of these in more detail below.

Conformity: Conformity is the most common type of social influence, and by now you probably know that conformity is when the individual adopts beliefs and behaviors in order to fit in with the ingroup.[lxxxiii] One of the most common forms of conformity people experience is peer pressure.

<u>Minority Influence</u>: Minority influence occurs when a majority is influenced to take on the beliefs and behaviors of a minority. There are numerous factors that can affect how this takes place, such as the influence of the minority and their social status.[lxxxiv] An example of this would be majority suburban kids who take on the persona of minority urban kids due to their influence in the entertainment industry.

<u>Reactance</u>: Reactance is the opposite of conformity. This is an outright rejection of the common beliefs and behaviors needed to fit in.[lxxxv] Have you seen the movie *Ten Things I Hate About You*, which is a modern day retelling of William Shakespeare's *The Taming of the Shrew*? In the film, Julia Stiles's character, Kat, is deeply in reactance. She will not date any of the boys at her high school, she thinks the rules and norms at her high school are stupid, and she overall cannot wait to graduate and go to college far, far away from the losers she has to go to school with.

<u>Obedience</u>: This is influence that comes from an authority figure or perceived authority

figure.[lxxxvi] Both the Stanford Prison Experiment and Milgram's Shock Experiments are studies in obedience.

Persuasion: Persuasion is appealing to reason or emotion through either logical or symbolic means to convince others to change their beliefs or behavior.[lxxxvii]

Psychological Manipulation: This is the use of deceptive practices in order to change beliefs and behavior. Psychological manipulation often uses abusive and underhanded tactics.[lxxxviii] Narcissists are often great psychological manipulators. They will often begin relationships by "love bombing," where they bombard their partner with attention and time and perhaps gifts, only to then disappear without a word, giving their partner the cold shoulder with no explanation as to why.

Abusive Power and Control: The person who uses abusive power and control uses a variety of tactics, like isolation, intimidation, or blaming, to maintain their power and influence over others so they will not have equal say in the relationship. Think of this as a classic domestic abuse situation. The abuser may prevent the abused from seeing or talking to friends and family so the abused becomes completely dependent on the abusive partner.[lxxxix] The abusive partner may blame the abused partner for the abuse, saying it's the other partner's fault for making the abuser angry, or the abuser may threaten to harm the abused partner if they leave the relationship.

Propaganda: Propaganda is the use of misinformation, particularly inflammatory misinformation, to trigger an emotional response to affect behavior and beliefs in others.[xc] One example of propaganda is the recruitment posters used during World War I as the United States encouraged men to enlist in the armed forces. One of these is the famous I Want You print bearing the image of Uncle Sam, calling all eligible men to sign up to fight. Many others were painted by Howard Chandler Christy and brought him national recognition. One of my personal favorites is the image of a young woman in a sailor suit with the words, "Gee, I wish I were a man. I'd join the Navy! Be a man and do it! Join the Navy."

Hard Power: This is the use of military or economic power against others of lesser military or economic power in order to get others to do what you want them to do.[xci] In 1991, the government of Somalia toppled due to infighting and unpopularity. This created a power vacuum in the country and various warlords all fought for power, and one technique many of them used was famine. This was a manmade famine used as a tool against Somalians to exert power and control over the Somali people while they slowly died of starvation. When other nations sent aid to help the drastic situation, the warlords confiscated the food for their own militia.

Case Study: Motivational Malleability[xcii]

In this study, researchers measured whether frontal cortical symmetry related to the susceptibility of social influence. Prior research has shown that frontal cortical asymmetry to the left has a disposition that allows individuals to increase their social influence. In contrast, individuals with asymmetry to the right will take actions that steer them away from risky choices. Based on this information and other neurophysiological data, higher activity in the right of the PFC should mean the individual is more likely to conform to societal norms. With this study, the researchers hypothesized that finding a pattern in PFC activity would show three things: it would show that complex behavior could be predicted; it would validate emerging research that social influence is truly about avoidance; and it would confirm the idea that individual differences and not just situations influence individual beliefs and behavior.

Results of the study confirmed that the researchers were correct. They first measured for conformity and found that conformity was strongly indicated in the experimental group, and in some cases of group participation, unanimous. When the researchers then measured the participants' brain activity in the PFC via an EEG, there was a consistent pattern of behavior that found right-side activity to be strongly affiliated with high levels of conformity. It should be noted that the researchers could only measure behavioral conformity, as they had no way to truly measure the individual's thoughts and beliefs.

The study also showed that other locations of the PFC were not associated with conformity. This information led the researchers to determine that many of the reasons a person chooses to conform to societal norms is due to their desire to avoid negative responses. This confirms the neuroscientific literature to date, that social influence, particularly influence that results in a negative response, is a powerful motivator that leads to conforming behavior.

Closing

This book has helped you look at how our brains process and interpret social interaction, but also how we are influenced by social interactions as well. As individuals, we all like to think we are stout in our beliefs and that no matter what, we would never be swayed from those core beliefs that define who we are as a person. However, social psychology tells us it's possible, and more than that, it has happened before in the modern era. Sometimes people have done things for survival, but neuroscience tells us humans are easily swayed by conformity and the need to fit in to avoid the consequences of societal punishment. Can you think of anything you do on a daily basis to avoid shunning or social ostracism? I can. I...

1. Use deodorant every day because no one wants to smell stinky armpits.

2. I shave every day and dress in a suit as it's considered professional where I work.
3. I don't walk into a store with no shoes on because, as they say, no shirt, no shoes, no service.
4. I don't pass gas as I walk down the hallway so everyone else knows it was Taco Tuesday yesterday.
5. I don't scream profanity at service workers because they are service workers and I am unhappy with the service provided. Although YouTube seems to show people doing this more and more frequently, I will never ever do this. I used to be a service worker.

From the top of my head, there are five things I do in order to fit in so that I don't stand out and receive negative feedback from my peers or society at large. Here are five negative responses one might receive in response to actions above.

1. No one will tolerate your presence because you stink.
2. You get a negative performance review because you don't dress professionally.
3. You can't get served at the establishment for being underdressed.
4. On Wednesdays, everyone in the hallway takes cover as you approach and then sprays Febreeze as you leave.
5. A service worker might spit in your food, not give that 25% off coupon they know about but you don't, or go the extra mile for you in any way they can to make your experience better.

So as you can see, even the most inane of social behaviors are driven by a desire to avoid negative consequences and to be a successful person in a world of different kinds of people. We automatically look for a way to connect to others and create an ingroup.

I encourage you to remember this message and to look for commonalities in others versus ways in which you are different. Look for ways you can understand different behaviors and not be judgmental toward others. Remember that many, many aspects of thoughts, beliefs, actions, and behaviors are a product of social influence. Don't try and change another person. If changing benefits another person, their brain will help them conduct a cost-benefit analysis and social influence will lead them to change all on their own.

Best,

A. R.

Reference

Aftanas, LI; Golocheikine, SA (September 2001). "Human anterior and frontal midline theta and lower alpha reflect emotionally positive state and internalized attention: high-resolution EEG investigation of meditation". Neuroscience Letters. 310 (1): 57–60. doi:10.1016/S0304-3940(01)02094-8. PMID 11524157.

Aronson, Elliot, Timothy D. Wilson, and Robin M. Akert. Social Psychology. Upper Saddle River, NJ: Prentice Hall, 2010. Print.

BC Campus. Thinking Like a Social Psychologist about Cooperation and Competition. Bc Campus. 2020. https://opentextbc.ca/socialpsychology/chapter/thinking-like-a-social-psychologist-about-cooperation-and-competition/

Blass, Thomas (1999). "The Milgram paradigm after 35 years: Some things we now know about obedience to authority". Journal of Applied Social Psychology. 29 (5): 955–978. doi:10.1111/j.1559-1816.1999.tb00134.x. as PDF Archived March 31, 2012.

Cacioppo J.T.; et al. (2007). "Social neuroscience: progress and implications for mental health". Perspectives on Psychological Science. 2 (2): 99–123. CiteSeerX 10.1.1.708.774. doi:10.1111/j.1745-6916.2007.00032.x. PMID 26151956.

Diagnostic and Statistical Manual of Mental Disorders, 5th Edition (DSM-5)

Foster, JJ; Sutterer, DW; Serences, JT; Vogel, EK; Awh, E (July 2017). "Alpha-Band Oscillations Enable Spatially and Temporally Resolved Tracking of Covert Spatial Attention". Psychological Science. 28 (7): 929–941.

Hiltunen T1, Kantola J, Abou Elseoud A, Lepola P, Suominen K, Starck T, Nikkinen J,

Remes J, Tervonen O, Palva S, Kiviniemi V, Palva JM. (2014). "Infra-slow EEG fluctuations are correlated with resting-state network dynamics in fMRI". [Article]. The Journal of Neuroscience, 34(2): 356-362.

John T. Cacioppo; Gary G. Berntson (1992). "Social psychological contributions to the decade of the brain: Doctrine of multilevel analysis". American Psychologist. 47 (8): 1019–1028. doi:10.1037/0003-066x.47.8.1019. PMID 1510329.

John T. Cacioppo; Gary G. Berntson; Jean Decety (2010). "Social neuroscience and its relation to social psychology". Social Cognition. 28 (6): 675–685. doi:10.1521/soco.2010.28.6.675. PMC 3883133. PMID 24409007.

Kean, Sam (May 6, 2014). "Phineas Gage, Neuroscience's Most Famous Patient". Slate. open access Reprinted in Skloot, Rebecca, ed. (2015). The Best American Science and Nature.

Lieberman, Matthew D. (2010), "Social Cognitive Neuroscience", Handbook of Social Psychology, American Cancer Society, doi:10.1002/9780470561119.socpsy001005, ISBN 9780470561119

Society for Social Neuroscience. Mission. Society for Social Neuroscience. 2020. https://www.s4sn.org/mission

Krauss Whitbourne, Susan. In-Groups, Out-Groups, and the Psychology of Crowds. Psychology Today. 2010. https://www.psychologytoday.com/us/blog/fulfillment-any-age/201012/in-groups-out-groups-and-the-psychology-crowds

Llinas, R. R. (2014). "Intrinsic electrical properties of mammalian neurons and CNS function: a historical perspective". Front Cell Neurosci. 8: 320. doi:10.3389/fncel.2014.00320. PMC 4219458. PMID 25408634.

McDermott B, Porter E, Hughes D, McGinley B, Lang M, O'Halloran M, Jones M. (2018). "Gamma Band Neural Stimulation in Humans and the Promise of a New Modality to Prevent and Treat Alzheimer's Disease". J Alzheimers Dis. 65 (2): 363–392. doi:10.3233/JAD-180391. PMC 6130417. PMID 30040729.

McLoad, Saul. Social Identity Theory. Simply Psychology. 2019. https://www.simplypsychology.org/social-identity-theory.html

McLoad, Saul. The Stanford Prison Experiment. Simply Psychology. 2020. https://www.simplypsychology.org/zimbardo.html

Radford, Benjamin. Critical Thinking Approaches To Confronting Racism. Skeptical Inquirer. 2018. https://skepticalinquirer.org/2018/01/critical-thinking-approaches-to-confronting-racism/

Rangaswamy M, Porjesz B, Chorlian DB, Wang K, Jones KA, Bauer LO, Rohrbaugh J, O'Connor SJ, Kuperman S, Reich T, Begleiter (2002). "Beta power in the EEG of alcoholics". Biological Psychology. 52 (8):

831–842. doi:10.1016/s0006-3223(02)01362-8. PMID 12372655.

Robert P. Abelson, Kurt P. Frey, Aiden P. Gregg: Experiments With People: Revelations from Social Psychology, Lawrence Elbaum Associates, Mahwah, NJ, 2003. ISBN 0-8058-2897-4

Sage Edge. Social Influence: Conformity, Social Roles, and Obedience. Social Psychology. 2020. https://us.sagepub.com/sites/default/files/07_h einzen_social_influence_0.pdf

Schnitzler A, Gross J (2005). "Normal and pathological oscillatory communication in the brain". Nature Reviews Neuroscience. 6 (4): 285–296. doi:10.1038/nrn1650. PMID 15803160.

Schnuerch, Robert & Pfattheicher, Stefan. (2017). Motivated Malleability: Frontal Cortical Asymmetry Predicts the Susceptibility to Social Influence. Social Neuroscience. 13. 10.1080/17470919.2017.1355333.

Serge Moscovici; Ivana Marková (2006). The Making of Modern Social Psychology. Cambridge: Polity Press. ISBN 9780745629667. ISBN 0-745-62966-0; ISBN 978-0-745-62966-7.

Vaughn, D. A., Savjani, R. R., Cohen, M. S., & Eagleman, D. M. (2018). Empathic Neural Responses Predict Group Allegiance. Frontiers in human neuroscience, 12, 302. https://doi.org/10.3389/fnhum.2018.00302

Xie, Yanni & Zhong, Chunyan & Zhang, Fangqing & Wu, Qi. (2019). The Ingroup Disadvantage in the Recognition of Micro-Expressions. 1-5. 10.1109/FG.2019.8756533.

Wang, Y., Meister, D. B., and Gray, P. H. 2013. "Social Influence and Knowledge Management Systems Use: Evidence from Panel Data," MIS Quarterly, (37:1), pp. 299-313.

Wolf Facts. Wolf Pack Hierarchy. Wolf Facts. 2020. http://wolffacts.org/wolf-pack-hierarchy.html

Wood, W.; Lundgren, S.; Ouellette, J.; Busceme, S. & Blackstone, T. (1994). "Minority Influence: A Meta-Analytic Review of Social Influence Processes". Psychological Bulletin. 115 (3): 323–345. doi:10.1037/0033-2909.115.3.323. PMID 8016284.

Endnotes

[i] John T. Cacioppo; Gary G. Berntson (1992). "Social psychological contributions to the decade of the brain: Doctrine of multilevel analysis". American Psychologist. 47 (8): 1019–1028. doi:10.1037/0003-066x.47.8.1019. PMID 1510329.

[ii] Wolf Facts. Wolf Pack Hierarchy. Wolf Facts. 2020. http://wolffacts.org/wolf-pack-hierarchy.html

[iii] Diagnostic and Statistical Manual of Mental Disorders, 5th Edition (DSM-5)

[iv] Society for Social Neuroscience. Mission. Society for Social Neuroscience. 2020. https://www.s4sn.org/mission

[v] Lieberman, Matthew D. (2010), "Social Cognitive Neuroscience", Handbook of Social Psychology, American Cancer Society, doi:10.1002/9780470561119.socpsy001005, ISBN 9780470561119

[vi] Kean, Sam (May 6, 2014). "Phineas Gage, Neuroscience's Most Famous Patient". Slate. open access Reprinted in Skloot, Rebecca, ed. (2015). The Best American Science and Nature

Writing 2015. Houghton Mifflin Harcourt. pp. 143–48.

[vii] Kean, Sam (May 6, 2014). "Phineas Gage, Neuroscience's Most Famous Patient". Slate. open access Reprinted in Skloot, Rebecca, ed. (2015). The Best American Science and Nature.

[viii] Society for Social Neuroscience. Mission. Society for Social Neuroscience. 2020. https://www.s4sn.org/mission

[ix] Lieberman, Matthew D. (2010), "Social Cognitive Neuroscience", Handbook of Social Psychology, American Cancer Society, doi:10.1002/9780470561119.socpsy001005, ISBN 9780470561119

[x] Lieberman, Matthew D. (2010), "Social Cognitive Neuroscience", Handbook of Social Psychology, American Cancer Society, doi:10.1002/9780470561119.socpsy001005, ISBN 9780470561119

[xi] Lieberman, Matthew D. (2010), "Social Cognitive Neuroscience", Handbook of Social Psychology, American Cancer Society, doi:10.1002/9780470561119.socpsy001005, ISBN 9780470561119

[xii] Llinas, R. R. (2014). "Intrinsic electrical properties of mammalian neurons and CNS function: a historical perspective". Front Cell Neurosci. 8: 320. doi:10.3389/fncel.2014.00320. PMC 4219458. PMID 25408634.

[xiii] Lieberman, Matthew D. (2010), "Social Cognitive Neuroscience", Handbook of Social Psychology, American Cancer Society, doi:10.1002/9780470561119.socpsy001005, ISBN 9780470561119

[xiv] Lieberman, Matthew D. (2010), "Social Cognitive Neuroscience", Handbook of Social Psychology, American Cancer Society, doi:10.1002/9780470561119.socpsy001005, ISBN 9780470561119

[xv] Schnitzler A, Gross J (2005). "Normal and pathological oscillatory communication in the brain". Nature Reviews Neuroscience. 6 (4): 285–296. doi:10.1038/nrn1650. PMID 15803160.

[xvi] Hiltunen T1, Kantola J, Abou Elseoud A, Lepola P, Suominen K, Starck T, Nikkinen J, Remes J, Tervonen O, Palva S, Kiviniemi V, Palva JM. (2014). "Infra-slow EEG fluctuations are correlated with resting-state network dynamics in fMRI". [Article]. The Journal of Neuroscience, 34(2): 356-362.

[xvii] Aftanas, LI; Golocheikine, SA (September 2001). "Human anterior and frontal midline theta and lower alpha reflect emotionally positive state and internalized attention: high-resolution EEG investigation of meditation". Neuroscience Letters. 310 (1): 57–60. doi:10.1016/S0304-3940(01)02094-8. PMID 11524157.

[xviii] Foster, JJ; Sutterer, DW; Serences, JT; Vogel, EK; Awh, E (July 2017). "Alpha-Band Oscillations Enable Spatially and Temporally Resolved Tracking of Covert Spatial Attention". Psychological Science. 28 (7): 929–941.

[xix] Rangaswamy M, Porjesz B, Chorlian DB, Wang K, Jones KA, Bauer LO, Rohrbaugh J, O'Connor SJ, Kuperman S, Reich T, Begleiter (2002). "Beta power in the EEG of alcoholics". Biological Psychology. 52 (8): 831–842. doi:10.1016/s0006-3223(02)01362-8. PMID 12372655.

[xx] McDermott B, Porter E, Hughes D, McGinley B, Lang M, O'Halloran M, Jones M. (2018). "Gamma Band Neural Stimulation in Humans and the Promise of a New Modality to Prevent and Treat Alzheimer's Disease". J Alzheimers Dis. 65 (2): 363–392. doi:10.3233/JAD-180391. PMC 6130417. PMID 30040729.

[xxi] John T. Cacioppo; Gary G. Berntson; Jean Decety (2010). "Social neuroscience and its relation to social psychology". Social Cognition. 28 (6): 675–685. doi:10.1521/soco.2010.28.6.675. PMC 3883133. PMID 24409007.

[xxii] John T. Cacioppo; Gary G. Berntson; Jean Decety (2010). "Social neuroscience and its relation to social psychology". Social Cognition. 28 (6): 675–685. doi:10.1521/soco.2010.28.6.675. PMC 3883133. PMID 24409007.

[xxiii] John T. Cacioppo; Gary G. Berntson; Jean Decety (2010). "Social neuroscience and its relation to social psychology". Social Cognition. 28 (6): 675–685. doi:10.1521/soco.2010.28.6.675. PMC 3883133. PMID 24409007.

[xxiv] John T. Cacioppo; Gary G. Berntson; Jean Decety (2010). "Social neuroscience and its relation to social psychology". Social Cognition. 28 (6): 675–685. doi:10.1521/soco.2010.28.6.675. PMC 3883133. PMID 24409007.

[xxv] John T. Cacioppo; Gary G. Berntson; Jean Decety (2010). "Social neuroscience and its relation to social psychology". Social Cognition. 28 (6): 675–685. doi:10.1521/soco.2010.28.6.675. PMC 3883133. PMID 24409007.

[xxvi] John T. Cacioppo; Gary G. Berntson; Jean Decety (2010). "Social neuroscience and its relation to social psychology". Social Cognition. 28 (6): 675–685. doi:10.1521/soco.2010.28.6.675. PMC 3883133. PMID 24409007.

[xxvii] John T. Cacioppo; Gary G. Berntson; Jean Decety (2010). "Social neuroscience and its relation to social psychology". Social Cognition. 28 (6): 675–685. doi:10.1521/soco.2010.28.6.675. PMC 3883133. PMID 24409007.

[xxviii] John T. Cacioppo; Gary G. Berntson; Jean Decety (2010). "Social neuroscience and its relation to social psychology". Social Cognition. 28

(6): 675–685. doi:10.1521/soco.2010.28.6.675.
PMC 3883133. PMID 24409007.

xxix John T. Cacioppo; Gary G. Berntson; Jean
Decety (2010). "Social neuroscience and its
relation to social psychology". Social Cognition. 28
(6): 675–685. doi:10.1521/soco.2010.28.6.675.
PMC 3883133. PMID 24409007.

xxx John T. Cacioppo; Gary G. Berntson; Jean
Decety (2010). "Social neuroscience and its
relation to social psychology". Social Cognition. 28
(6): 675–685. doi:10.1521/soco.2010.28.6.675.
PMC 3883133. PMID 24409007.

xxxi John T. Cacioppo; Gary G. Berntson; Jean
Decety (2010). "Social neuroscience and its
relation to social psychology". Social Cognition. 28
(6): 675–685. doi:10.1521/soco.2010.28.6.675.
PMC 3883133. PMID 24409007.

xxxii John T. Cacioppo; Gary G. Berntson; Jean
Decety (2010). "Social neuroscience and its
relation to social psychology". Social Cognition. 28
(6): 675–685. doi:10.1521/soco.2010.28.6.675.
PMC 3883133. PMID 24409007.

xxxiii John T. Cacioppo; Gary G. Berntson; Jean
Decety (2010). "Social neuroscience and its
relation to social psychology". Social Cognition. 28
(6): 675–685. doi:10.1521/soco.2010.28.6.675.
PMC 3883133. PMID 24409007.

xxxiv John T. Cacioppo; Gary G. Berntson; Jean
Decety (2010). "Social neuroscience and its

relation to social psychology". Social Cognition. 28 (6): 675–685. doi:10.1521/soco.2010.28.6.675. PMC 3883133. PMID 24409007.

[xxxv] Cacioppo J.T.; et al. (2007). "Social neuroscience: progress and implications for mental health". Perspectives on Psychological Science. 2 (2): 99–123. CiteSeerX 10.1.1.708.774. doi:10.1111/j.1745-6916.2007.00032.x. PMID 26151956.

[xxxvi] Cacioppo J.T.; et al. (2007). "Social neuroscience: progress and implications for mental health". Perspectives on Psychological Science. 2 (2): 99–123. CiteSeerX 10.1.1.708.774. doi:10.1111/j.1745-6916.2007.00032.x. PMID 26151956.

[xxxvii] Cacioppo J.T.; et al. (2007). "Social neuroscience: progress and implications for mental health". Perspectives on Psychological Science. 2 (2): 99–123. CiteSeerX 10.1.1.708.774. doi:10.1111/j.1745-6916.2007.00032.x. PMID 26151956.

[xxxviii] Robert P. Abelson, Kurt P. Frey, Aiden P. Gregg: Experiments With People: Revelations from Social Psychology, Lawrence Elbaum Associates, Mahwah, NJ, 2003. ISBN 0-8058-2897-4

[xxxix] BC Campus. Thinking Like a Social Psychologist about Cooperation and Competition. Bc Campus. 2020.

https://opentextbc.ca/socialpsychology/chapter/thinking-like-a-social-psychologist-about-cooperation-and-competition/

[xl] Balconi, M., Vanutelli, M. (2017) Brains in Competition: Improved cognitive performance and inter-brain coupling by hyperscanning paradigm with Near-Infrared Spectroscopy. Frontiers of Behavioral Neuroscience. August 2017

[xli] Balconi, M., Vanutelli, M. (2017) Brains in Competition: Improved cognitive performance and inter-brain coupling by hyperscanning paradigm with Near-Infrared Spectroscopy. Frontiers of Behavioral Neuroscience. August 2017

[xlii] Balconi, M., Crivelli, D., Vanutelli, M. (2017) Why to Cooperate is Better than to Compete: Brain and personality components. BioMed Central Neuroscience.

[xliii] Balconi, M., Crivelli, D., Vanutelli, M. (2017) Why to Cooperate is Better than to Compete: Brain and personality components. BioMed Central Neuroscience.

[xliv] Balconi, M., Crivelli, D., Vanutelli, M. (2017) Why to Cooperate is Better than to Compete: Brain and personality components. BioMed Central Neuroscience.

[xlv] Balconi, M., Crivelli, D., Vanutelli, M. (2017) Why to Cooperate is Better than to Compete:

Brain and personality components. BioMed
Central Neuroscience.

[xlvi] Balconi, M., Crivelli, D., Vanutelli, M. (2017)
Why to Cooperate is Better than to Compete:
Brain and personality components. BioMed
Central Neuroscience.

[xlvii] Paradies, Y., Priest, N., Ben, J., Truong, M.,
Gupta, A., Pieterse, A., Kelaher, M., Gilbert, G.
(2013) Racism as a Determinant of Health: A
protocol for conducting systematic review and
meta-analysis. Systematic Reviews, vol 2, no. 85,
pp 1-7.

[xlviii] Paradies, Y. (2016) Racism and Health
Reference Module in Biomedical Sciences, ch 5,
pp 1-13.

[xlix] Paradies, Y. (2016) Racism and Health
Reference Module in Biomedical Sciences, ch 5,
pp 1-13.

[l] Radford, Benjamin. Critical Thinking Approaches
To Confronting Racism. Skeptical Inquirer. 2018.
https://skepticalinquirer.org/2018/01/critical-
thinking-approaches-to-confronting-racism/

[li] Serge Moscovici; Ivana Marková (2006). The
Making of Modern Social Psychology. Cambridge:
Polity Press. ISBN 9780745629667. ISBN 0-745-
62966-0; ISBN 978-0-745-62966-7.

[lii] McLoad, Saul. Social Identity Theory. Simply
Psychology. 2019.

https://www.simplypsychology.org/social-identity-theory.html

[liii] McLoad, Saul. Social Identity Theory. Simply Psychology. 2019.
https://www.simplypsychology.org/social-identity-theory.html

[liv] McLoad, Saul. Social Identity Theory. Simply Psychology. 2019.
https://www.simplypsychology.org/social-identity-theory.html

[lv] McLoad, Saul. Social Identity Theory. Simply Psychology. 2019.
https://www.simplypsychology.org/social-identity-theory.html

[lvi] McLoad, Saul. Social Identity Theory. Simply Psychology. 2019.
https://www.simplypsychology.org/social-identity-theory.html

[lvii] McLoad, Saul. Social Identity Theory. Simply Psychology. 2019.
https://www.simplypsychology.org/social-identity-theory.html

[lviii] Krauss Whitbourne, Susan. In-Groups, Out-Groups, and the Psychology of Crowds. Psychology Today. 2010.
https://www.psychologytoday.com/us/blog/fulfillment-any-age/201012/in-groups-out-groups-and-the-psychology-crowds

[lix] Vaughn, D. A., Savjani, R. R., Cohen, M. S., & Eagleman, D. M. (2018). Empathic Neural Responses Predict Group Allegiance. Frontiers in human neuroscience, 12, 302. https://doi.org/10.3389/fnhum.2018.00302

[lx] Vaughn, D. A., Savjani, R. R., Cohen, M. S., & Eagleman, D. M. (2018). Empathic Neural Responses Predict Group Allegiance. Frontiers in human neuroscience, 12, 302. https://doi.org/10.3389/fnhum.2018.00302

[lxi] Vaughn, D. A., Savjani, R. R., Cohen, M. S., & Eagleman, D. M. (2018). Empathic Neural Responses Predict Group Allegiance. Frontiers in human neuroscience, 12, 302. https://doi.org/10.3389/fnhum.2018.00302

[lxii] Vaughn, D. A., Savjani, R. R., Cohen, M. S., & Eagleman, D. M. (2018). Empathic Neural Responses Predict Group Allegiance. Frontiers in human neuroscience, 12, 302. https://doi.org/10.3389/fnhum.2018.00302

[lxiii] Vaughn, D. A., Savjani, R. R., Cohen, M. S., & Eagleman, D. M. (2018). Empathic Neural Responses Predict Group Allegiance. Frontiers in human neuroscience, 12, 302. https://doi.org/10.3389/fnhum.2018.00302

[lxiv] Vaughn, D. A., Savjani, R. R., Cohen, M. S., & Eagleman, D. M. (2018). Empathic Neural Responses Predict Group Allegiance. Frontiers in

Psychology. 29 (5): 955–978. doi:10.1111/j.1559-1816.1999.tb00134.x. as PDF Archived March 31, 2012

[lxxviii] Sage Edge. Social Influence: Conformity, Social Roles, and Obedience. Social Psychology. 2020. https://us.sagepub.com/sites/default/files/07_heinzen_social_influence_0.pdf

[lxxix] Wang, Y., Meister, D. B., and Gray, P. H. 2013. "Social Influence and Knowledge Management Systems Use: Evidence from Panel Data," MIS Quarterly, (37:1), pp. 299-313.

[lxxx] Wang, Y., Meister, D. B., and Gray, P. H. 2013. "Social Influence and Knowledge Management Systems Use: Evidence from Panel Data," MIS Quarterly, (37:1), pp. 299-313.

[lxxxi] Wang, Y., Meister, D. B., and Gray, P. H. 2013. "Social Influence and Knowledge Management Systems Use: Evidence from Panel Data," MIS Quarterly, (37:1), pp. 299-313.

[lxxxii] Wang, Y., Meister, D. B., and Gray, P. H. 2013. "Social Influence and Knowledge Management Systems Use: Evidence from Panel Data," MIS Quarterly, (37:1), pp. 299-313.

[lxxxiii] Wood, W.; Lundgren, S.; Ouellette, J.; Busceme, S. & Blackstone, T. (1994). "Minority Influence: A Meta-Analytic Review of Social Influence Processes". Psychological Bulletin. 115

(3): 323–345. doi:10.1037/0033-2909.115.3.323. PMID 8016284.

[lxxxiv] Wood, W.; Lundgren, S.; Ouellette, J.; Busceme, S. & Blackstone, T. (1994). "Minority Influence: A Meta-Analytic Review of Social Influence Processes". Psychological Bulletin. 115 (3): 323–345. doi:10.1037/0033-2909.115.3.323. PMID 8016284.

[lxxxv] Aronson, Elliot, Timothy D. Wilson, and Robin M. Akert. Social Psychology. Upper Saddle River, NJ: Prentice Hall, 2010. Print.

[lxxxvi] Wood, W.; Lundgren, S.; Ouellette, J.; Busceme, S. & Blackstone, T. (1994). "Minority Influence: A Meta-Analytic Review of Social Influence Processes". Psychological Bulletin. 115 (3): 323–345. doi:10.1037/0033-2909.115.3.323. PMID 8016284.

[lxxxvii] Aronson, Elliot, Timothy D. Wilson, and Robin M. Akert. Social Psychology. Upper Saddle River, NJ: Prentice Hall, 2010. Print.

[lxxxviii] Aronson, Elliot, Timothy D. Wilson, and Robin M. Akert. Social Psychology. Upper Saddle River, NJ: Prentice Hall, 2010. Print.

[lxxxix] Aronson, Elliot, Timothy D. Wilson, and Robin M. Akert. Social Psychology. Upper Saddle River, NJ: Prentice Hall, 2010. Print.

[xc] Aronson, Elliot, Timothy D. Wilson, and Robin M. Akert. Social Psychology. Upper Saddle River, NJ: Prentice Hall, 2010. Print.

[xci] Aronson, Elliot, Timothy D. Wilson, and Robin M. Akert. Social Psychology. Upper Saddle River, NJ: Prentice Hall, 2010. Print.

[xcii]Schnuerch, Robert & Pfattheicher, Stefan. (2017). Motivated Malleability: Frontal Cortical Asymmetry Predicts the Susceptibility to Social Influence. Social Neuroscience. 13. 10.1080/17470919.2017.1355333.